A Pint of Patience with a Dollop of Love

A Recipe for Parenting

By: Dr. Rachna Buxani-Mirpuri

A Molding Messengers Publication

A Pint of Patience with a Dollop of Love

Copyright © 2021 by Dr. Rachna Buxani-Mirpuri

For information about permission to reproduce selections from this book, Write to:

Molding Messengers, LLC

1728 NE Miami Gardens Dr, Suite #111, North Miami Beach, FL, 33179

or email Info.Staff@MoldingMessengers.com.

www.MoldingMessengers.com

Library of Congress Control Number: 2021909474

Print ISBN: 978-0-578-91364-3

eBook ISBN: 978-0-578-91365-0

A Molding Messengers Publication

A Pint of Patience with a Dollop of Love

A Recipe for Parenting

By: Dr. Rachna Buxani-Mirpuri

A Molding Messengers Publication

Dedication

With love for my mother, Veena Ram Buxani, I am not sure where you find the energy to be a constant rock of support and inspiration for my sisters and me. You have forever been gentle in your judgment, patient with your words, giving in your advice, and selfless in your prayers. I am as fortunate and enthusiastic as any child should be. You have shown me how to stretch my limits and step out of my comfort zones. As I pass on the estate of incalculable values, you taught me, I thank you. Mom your sacrifices are invaluable, so this book is affectionately your own.

I

FOREWORD

I poured my heart to impact the lives of others by expanding my circle of concern to include anyone able to read this book. I started out as a School counselor, where I worked with countless families in over 21 schools. My writing experience at Khaleej Times and Gulf News, daily English language newspapers published in Dubai, and my personal experiences as a daughter, a sister, a friend, and a therapist, inspired this book.

I never knew all the knowledge I acquired would one day turn into a recipe for a challenging job: Parenting. Over my fruitful career, I noticed that parents from all walks of life asked the same questions. Parenting requires shared wisdom, compassion, and understanding between parents, their children, and the world. I am confident that the first glimpse of the world for a child is through their parents' practices, communication patterns, and habits.

I will walk you through my thinking in this book as I share my parenting recipes and suggest ways to do it better. I introduce character development, conflict management, the power of uttering positivity, trusting your instincts, communication, and listening to your children attentively. I intuitively share about caring for each child while appreciating their uniqueness. I also remind every parent to shun comparison and to engage in practices of empathy, love, and unbiased support for their children.

This book will offer a valuable guide as it reflects on building strong, healthy relationships between parents and their children. It is humbling to learn and relearn concepts. I indeed acknowledge that parenting is a continuous process and does not require perfection, as shared by Kahlil Gibran in his poem:

"Your children are not your children.

They are sons and daughters of life's longing for itself.

They come through you but not from you.

And though they are with you yet, they belong not to you.

You may give them your love but not your thoughts, for they have their own thoughts.

You may house their bodies but not their souls, for their souls dwell in the house of tomorrow, which you cannot visit, not even in your dreams.

You may strive to be like them but seek not to make them like you. For life goes not backward nor tarries with yesterday.

You are the bows from which your children as living arrows are sent forth. The archer sees the make upon the path of the infinite, and He bends you with His might that His arrows may go swift and far.

Let your bending in the archer's hand be for gladness. For even as He loves the arrow that flies, so He also loves the bow that is stable."

My deepest gratitude to my family, my friends, and the editorial team. Your patience and support are forever appreciated. I hope this book is used as a resource to touch your lives and teach you fulfilling recipes of parenthood.

Table of Contents

Section 1: CHARACTER MATTERS

Build Your Child's Character

One night, I watched the wonderful movie "Frozen" with my two nieces. At the time, one was eleven years old, and the other was just about four. At about 9 p.m., my darling 4-year-old niece was feeling too sleepy and started squirming in her seat, petitioning me to take her home. I asked her would she mind staying a while longer since her older sister seemed to be enjoying the movie. Of course, being only four years old, I expected her to start whining and demanding to be taken home at that very instant, but this was far from true. She very thoughtfully agreed to sit through so her sister did not have to miss the movie. I was astounded by her response and later patted my sister on the back for doing such an excellent job in instilling the great character values of respect and care in her little angel.

Trustworthiness, Responsibility, Caring, Respect, Citizenship, and Fairness are some of the virtues all of us wish our children grow up with. Aristotle believed that humans are born to become virtuous, mature adults.

We live in a time when teaching our children to be virtuous is particularly challenging. Our youngsters are surrounded by false messages by advertisers and programming filled with violence and lies as a form of entertainment. If you feel overwhelmed as a parent in teaching your

1

children positive character traits like honesty, respect, humility, courage, and generosity, you are not alone!

Children are born with different temperaments, which explains why some children are timid while others are oozing with confidence and why some find it easier to share their toys than others. No matter a child's personality, all children have the potential of building in the character virtues that will ensure they become positive contributors to society.

"My daughter never shares her toys with others. What can I do to make her kind and generous with her friends?"

Over the years, I have heard numerous such concerns by parents struggling to bring up their children with the right values. Believe it or not, a lot of what your children will grow up to do will depend upon what they see you doing. The moral messages you provide your children must be clear, consistent, and repetitive. For example, as a parent, do not rationalize good virtues when you are tired, rushed, or under pressure.

Parents provide children with their first glimpses of courage, honesty, fairness, and respect.

One of the most powerful tools to build character blocks in children is to "catch them being respectful, courteous, and caring." Parents often focus on everything wrong their children are doing, forgetting to complement their good, virtuous behaviors. So, next time little Johnny decides to share his toys, bring an uncle a glass of water, or just maintain silence if someone wants to read, make sure you provide those two little words of encouragement. As a principle, children tend to repeat behaviors that get them attention, whether good or bad.

Character is also developed through practice.

Some things that you can do as a parent to be an example to your children are:

- Encourage your children to volunteer at their school or local organizations.
- If they are afraid of doing this alone, you can volunteer at local organizations along with your children.
- Be creative in teaching your children good character traits.
- Play games and role-play to help you in the process.
- Television programs and the news provide excellent opportunities to talk about good and destructive behaviors.
- You could also have a money bank where the whole family could put in some money every month and send it to a local charity.

In the past, success in our society was defined by character and human values. Unfortunately, this has been replaced by achievement and performance. When people come to the fork on the road of life where they must choose either character or achievement, they often choose the latter. The society we live in today is the most informed and well-educated society by far, yet sadly, vices of smoking, alcohol, stealing, and lying are on the rise among our youth. More parents are becoming anxious and fretful than ever before, wondering whether their child will grow up to be a good citizen with the proper morals or follow a path of self-destruction.

Children of character know within their heart that it is "cool" to say "NO" to the ills that society has to offer. They will **not** be easily influenced into doing wrong when mom and dad have taught them "good character traits." So, let us join hands in ensuring we are bringing up a whole genre of individuals who are not solely driven by money or power but by a strong belief system of right and wrong!

In the words of Theodore Roosevelt, "Character, in the long run, is the decisive factor in the life of an individual and of nations alike."

Character Development in Children

When it comes to character development, your children first need to see virtue in action to try out their virtue wings. Parents, relatives, siblings, and childcare providers give their first glimpses of courage, honesty, generosity, fairness, and respect. It is not enough for your children to see you and other significant family members and peers behaving virtuously; they also need encouragement, praise, and character feedback.

You can encourage your children with words or simply by showing faith in positive potential. For the boy who is acting selfish, you might say,

"I am going to stop reminding you to share since I know you can do it yourself."

Practice actively noticing your child's behavior when they do something positive. For example, when you see your daughter share her toys with her friends, you might just say, "Hey, I noticed you let Joanna play with your special toy." You do not even need to follow that comment up with praise because just the fact that you noticed will have a positive effect on them.

Children will repeat actions that get the attention of their parents.

We need to acknowledge our children more for doing good acts than reprimand them for misbehaving. Most parents find it natural to give negative character feedback to children. If a child is easily angered and reactive, we forget that she is only sometimes angry and mean, but we tend to say, "Why do you have to be so mean?"

Unfortunately, when we repeatedly focus on children's negatives, they tend to begin believing us. So, the girl who acts angry begins to define herself as an angry girl. Thus, it is essential instead to notice when your children behave kindly and to say something positive and character-building such as, "You are a girl who knows how to be nice to her friends."

Character development is enhanced by opportunities to do good in the world.

Volunteering to help at food banks, helping coach younger children, giving money to a family chosen charity all instill important habits in your children. Character development begins at home and continues at school. As a parent, consider how you can bring some of your best character-building ideas to your child's school. You can have a voice in encouraging the school to choose character-building reading materials and speakers. Talk to your child's school counselor, teachers, coaches, and principal about how you can contribute to the challenge of character development in all young people!

Encourage Children to Help Them Succeed

Criticism often discourages children from trying.

"You will always be a failure because you never know how to take care of your things."

"You will never succeed in life if you behave like such a klutz!"

Parents often try to get their children to behave in a certain way by pointing out what they are not doing correctly or criticizing them. Mrs. Dawson came to me distressed with her ten-year-old daughter Alyssa for not being responsible. She claimed that all efforts to teach the right behaviors in the child were in vain. When asked about how she handled the situation, I realized that most of her disciplining tactics involved nagging and ridiculing Alyssa's actions. This was where the root of the problem lay. Alyssa had eventually learned how to turn a deaf ear to her mother's repeated criticisms. Thus, her actions were not improving.

Parents fail to realize this common tactic of criticizing children does not work.

So, what then can be done to improve the situation?

Encouraging children is a better approach. Find whatever good there is in a situation and mention that. This may seem impossible when the child's bedroom is an embarrassing sight or their grades have been falling because homework is not being turned in on time; however, recognition of good qualities motivates children to try harder. Recognizing their good qualities, in turn, enables them to improve.

Praise is one of the most powerful tools to help a child improve. Unfortunately, many parents believe the way to get children to do better is to criticize their poor performance. Parents need to adopt an alternative positive approach to achieve results.

Expecting too much too soon is counterproductive. It is essential to set appropriate goals for your child. Remember, you can break any skill into small segments and work at accomplishing each small part. Begin by expecting children to either make their bed or pick up their clothes. When the first task has been completed, add another. It is essential to encourage children by giving them tasks they can perform. If parents expect too much, it hampers development.

Nothing builds success like success. Children who are encouraged and who experience success will build on their experiences and enjoy even more success. The best way to help a child to build positive behaviors is through large doses of positive strokes. No matter how poor a child's performance, there are some things he is doing correctly. To best help children develop their skills, concentrate on what they do well.

Continually pushing children to do better without recognizing what they have already accomplished can result in them thinking that they will never be good enough! The wise parent knows when and how hard to encourage children without applying too much pressure.

Parents do not realize that constantly criticizing the child may result in the child developing feelings of inferiority and insecurity. A child must be given a good, positive, and healthy environment to grow and develop a sense of positive self-worth. A positive self-concept provides a cornerstone to helping children develop productive behaviors.

Praise is a tool we need to use to let children know we are excited about their achievements and the only means to help ensure they continue displaying these behaviors.

Some families give little attention or positive feedback, so it is a big step to learn to praise the children. However, one of the most important things we must do as parents is let our children know they are special no matter what!

Mirror, Mirror on the Wall

Dear Ms. Rachna,

I am so depressed. I want to look like the girls in fashion magazines, but that is far from true. It's not that I don't try. I have tried everything, including starving myself, rigorously exercising, trying out the beauty and hair tips mentioned, and even taking these miracle pills that seem to show results on the models. But I still end up looking like "ME," and I hate that. Please help me before I drive myself crazy about this!

From,

Ugly Fat Girl

During my years as a school counselor, I received numerous such emails from troubled children. Research suggests many adolescents are discontented with their bodies. I came across several elementary school-aged children who had already dieted at least once to lose weight because they thought they were too fat!

Body image is defined by what we feel about our physical appearance

and how we think others perceive us.

In today's media-driven world, where youth are constantly bombarded with messages and images of beauty ideals, it is no wonder we have an alarming number of them who feel bad about themselves and their bodies. Many feel they are not thin enough or muscular enough or tall enough or perfect enough! Children constantly compare themselves to others or to the images they see on TV or in magazines and end up feeling inadequate.

They allow the numbers on a weighing scale or a height chart to determine their self-esteem. In the past, more females seemed to be pushed to achieve the unrealistic cultural standards of beauty; however, nowadays, an increasing number of males are expected to conform to an ideal male look, as well.

Personal appearance is especially important to all of us. It affects how we interact with others, what we achieve in our lives, and most importantly, how we feel about ourselves. A negative body image results in poor self-esteem and can also result in our children developing life-threatening eating disorders.

So, how can parents help?

The family is very influential in how children end up feeling about themselves and their bodies.

Here are some pointers to assist parents in helping their children develop a positive body image.

The most effective practice that parents can engage in is to model a positive and healthy self-image. Your children listen to what you say, even though that may not seem to be the case sometimes. If you constantly complain and whine about your looks and weight, your children will be quick to catch on. Generally, parental acceptance of their bodies goes a long way in assuring children's approval of their bodies.

- Do not pass negative comments about food, weight, and body sizes.
- Do not tease or taunt your children about their physical characteristics.
- Do not compare your children to others. Cherish their unique differences and individuality.
- Encourage your children to develop wholesome eating habits and a good exercise routine to build a healthy relationship with their bodies.
- Talk to your children about how good looks come in all shapes, sizes, and colors.
- Help your children deal with negative thoughts about their looks. Teach them how to replace negative thoughts with more positive ones. For example, if your daughter comments, "I hate my hair," stop her immediately and ask her to replace it with one thing she loves about herself, like "I have nice eyes."

- Praise and encourage characteristics like intelligence, compassion, and generosity in your children to reduce the focus on appearances.
- Discuss the messages your children receive through the media and critically analyze them. Tell your children, contrary to what the advertisers want them to believe; people do not have perfect bodies, hair, teeth, skin, and so on. Also, shed light on the truth that models look the way they do with the help of lighting experts, hair and make-up artists.
- Stress on body changes that occur during puberty and how they are a normal part of growing and developing.
- Help your children broaden their definition of beauty by talking to them about how beauty ideals have changed over time. Also, speak to them about not judging others based on their physical appearances.
- Discuss with your children the goals and dreams they have for their lives and focus more on how they can work toward achieving these.

Children today live in a complex world dictated by personal and social challenges. Parents want the best for their children. We must strive toward helping our children recognize and fight the myth of "ideal" and "perfect" beauty and support them in developing a healthy, positive self-image.

"A strong, positive self-image is the best possible preparation for success in life."

-Dr. Joyce Brothers

Empowering Your Children to Develop a Healthy Self-Image

Once upon a time, a rabbit was passing through a forest and saw a fox nearby. "Oh, my goodness! A fox!" exclaimed the rabbit. "Foxes eat rabbits. I'd better hop away as fast as I can before he sees me and eats me up." So, the rabbit hopped away speedily. A second rabbit was walking past and saw the same fox. He thought, "Oh goodness a fox! Foxes eat rabbits. I'd better hop off before he sees me." However, being fearful and less confident, he thought, "But what if I can't hop away fast enough? What if the fox sees me and outruns me? What if there is no place for me to hide? What if…"CHOMP!

Children with good self-esteem are better able to face life's challenges and develop healthy relationships with themselves and others.

Self-esteem is what we think of ourselves and our abilities, along with our perception of what others think of us. It is our overall sense of personal effectiveness. Parents play a significant role in helping children develop a healthy self-image. How often do we forget to shower our children with little words of encouragement? Parents tend to overlook the impact words like "good job," "well-done," and "that was great" can have on their children.

Here are some pointers to help raise children with a positive image about themselves:

- Set fitting standards for your children and help them do the same for themselves. If unachievable standards are constantly set, it will ensure they feel discouraged.
- A survey done on adults with disabilities revealed that the one factor that encourages them to move on in life was the faith expressed in them by a caring adult. Belief in your child's abilities is one of the major driving forces for achieving success. Build your child's confidence to handle challenges by demonstrating your trust in his abilities.
- Praise is probably one of the most powerful tools in building your child's self-image. Focus on your child's strengths and successes rather than constantly pointing out his weaknesses and failures.
- One of the most common sources of discouragement is trying to do too much too fast. Teach your children that the longest of journeys start with a single step. Your child needs to approach challenges one step at a time not to feel overwhelmed by them.

- Do not criticize or ridicule your children. Target the behavior and not the child. Instead of saying something like, "You are so lazy. Your room looks like a pigsty. Can't you do anything right," use statements like, "I would like you to keep your clothes in your closet so that your room can look neater."

- Do not compare your children to others. I am sure you have heard this countless times, and still, parents cannot resist the temptation of commenting on their next-door neighbor's son's performance on the math test, which is much better than their son's. Comparing your child to his siblings or others is a sure-fire way of making him feel inadequate.

- Empower your child, so he may be successful in overcoming obstacles. Teach your child the art of positive self-talk. For example, a child who is stressed out for an exam can be taught to practice statements like, "I am well-prepared for the exam. I am going to do well on it." A child who has just lost a match could be taught to say, "It's alright if we did not win. We tried our best, and that's what matters." Negative self-talk results in children experiencing a lack of confidence.

- Help your children be able to laugh at themselves. Teach them life is not always that serious. A good sense of humor and an ability to make light of life are essential to help our children enjoy life!

Our children live in a complex and competitive world

where maintaining a positive outlook can be challenging.

Your child cannot ask for a life free from obstacles and risks. The key to riding through the storms successfully is acting with self-confidence. The story of the two rabbits highlights the importance of a healthy self-image in being able to cope effectively with the trials presented to us in our daily lives.

Thus, the recipe to our children's healthy self-image is:

➢ 1 ounce of love and affection
➢ 1 ounce of encouragement and praise
➢ 1 ounce of empowerment with positive self-talk
➢ 1 ounce of faith
➢ 1 cup of the ability to laugh at oneself!

Raising Kids with Healthy Self-Esteem

Healthy self-esteem is a child's armor against the challenges of the world. Kids who feel good about themselves seem to handle conflicts and resist negative pressures more easily. They tend to smile more and enjoy life.

Parents want their children to grow up with good self-esteem and feel that they are lovable and worthwhile individuals. Society's expectations today are exceedingly high for youngsters. Thus, it has become increasingly difficult for them to meet these standards and feel good about themselves. In my therapy sessions with teenagers, I frequently come across youth who feel the constant need to hide behind a mask and be someone who they are not to impress others or fit in. They are always afraid that their peers will not accept their true selves. As parents, we must ensure that our children grow up into healthy and confident adults by helping them through the challenging task of building and maintaining a good self-concept.

The first and most important thing for parents to do is listen to their children's thoughts and understand their emotions. Listening to your children with empathy tells them you care about what they think and feel.

The second principle is to create situations that will help your kids experience more success than failure. Do not set standards that are too high for them.

Praise your child for his efforts and give positive feedback. For example, if your child does not make the soccer team, avoid saying, "Well, next time, you'll work harder and make it." Instead, say, "Well, you didn't make the team, but I'm proud of the effort you put into it." You want your children to grow up with far more praise than criticism and more accomplishments than failures.

Combat your child's negative and irrational beliefs about himself with positive thoughts. For example, a child who does very well in school but struggles with math may say, "I can't do math. I'm a bad student." Not only is this a false generalization, but it is also a belief that will harm them. Encourage your child to see the situation in its true light. A helpful response might be: "You are a good student. You work hard in school. Math is a subject that you need to spend more time on. We'll work on it together."

As your children grow, they become increasingly sensitive to the evaluations of their peers. You can help them learn to build healthy relationships with their peers, which will help enhance their self-image.

Another way to strengthen self-esteem is to try and build upon a specific skill or ability. This may be in athletics, academics, music, or any special talent the child possesses. If your child does not appear to have a particular interest, expose her to different activities so that she can find her passion.

The next step is to give your children a certain amount of control over their lives. For example: When they are younger your kids can decide what they want to wear if it is appropriate, and when they are older, they can choose their course of study. If you control your kids too much, they might feel inadequate to handle their own lives, whereas too little control might make them feel that you do not care.

Always make your children feel that they are loved and cared for. Fill your children's lives with loving words and hugs. Your love will go a long way in boosting their self-esteem.

Finally, try to model healthy self-esteem in yourself. Research has shown that parents who have high self-esteem often have high self-esteem children. This is one of the more important principles since you cannot give to your children what you do not grant to yourself: self-love.

Parents can strengthen their children's self-esteem by treating them respectfully, placing value on their views and opinions, and expressing appreciation. Above all, parents must keep in mind that self-esteem is an integral part of every child's development. Take the time to teach, guide, and involve your child. We are the best chance they have.

Key Points

➤ Trustworthiness, Responsibility, Caring, Respect, Citizenship, and Fairness are some of the virtues all of us wish our children grow up with.

➤ Aristotle believed that humans are born to become virtuous, mature adults.

➤ Parents provide children with their first glimpses of courage, honesty, fairness, and respect.

➤ Character is developed through practice.

➤ In the words of Theodore Roosevelt, "Character, in the long run, is the decisive factor in the life of an individual and of nations alike."

➤ Children will repeat actions that get the attention of their parents.

➤ Character development is enhanced by opportunities to do good in the world.

➤ Criticism often discourages children from trying.

➤ Praise is a tool we need to use to let children know we are excited about their achievements and the only tool that helps ensure they continue displaying these behaviors.

➤ Self-image is defined by what we feel about our physical appearance and how we think others perceive us.

➤ Children with good self-esteem are better able to face life's challenges and develop healthy relationships with themselves and others.

➤ Our children live in a complex and competitive world where maintaining a positive outlook can be challenging.

➤ Dr. Joyce Brothers says, "A strong, positive self-image is the best possible preparation for success in life."

Section 2: Social and Emotional Skills

Helping Children Build Social Skills

Children need to learn relationship competencies such as taking turns, sharing, greetings, helping others, following directions, using kind words, sympathy for others, and more. Eight-year-old John has a tough time making and keeping friends. He is always displaying inappropriate behaviors like acting bossy, shouting at the other kids, and not sharing. His parents are overly concerned that John will grow up to be a very lonely child.

Building positive peer relations is

probably one of the most important developmental tasks

that a child must accomplish.

Healthy relationships with peers help a child build sound self-esteem and promote psychological well-being. On the other hand, unhealthy peer relations are a predictor of social, academic, or psychological problems in adolescence and adulthood.

Parents can help build healthy social skills in their children. First, start by identifying what your child's strengths and weaknesses are in their social skills so that you can develop a plan to help. Watch for signs including the child not being cooperative, not having many friends, being a poor loser, not understanding proper personal space, using a whiney, unfriendly, or loud voice, and being overly critical.

One strategy that works very well to help kids build social skills is "stop-think-act."

Ask your child to think before reacting to ensure appropriate behavior. Role-playing situations and demonstrating suitable reactions is a technique that can be adopted to help children. Another technique that is effective in this regard is problem-solving. List a problem situation and brainstorm appropriate solutions to deal with it. Also, it is helpful to teach your child proper ways of communicating, like using "I" statements and an appropriate tone of voice. This will help your child develop respect for others and feelings of empathy.

Parents can also help foster friendships by arranging for one-on-one playtimes with new friends, providing interactive toys, and teaching conversation openers.

Teach your child to embrace diversity. Teach them that difference is what makes their world a special and exciting place.

It is also vital for parents to teach their children how to handle rude people by staying calm and ignoring the behavior. Never give your child permission to hit another child. If necessary, teach your child to protect himself, but not to fight. Discuss alternative ways to resolve conflicts. Parents play a vital role in teaching their children appropriate social skills.

Psychologists suggest that social and emotional development are

equally important to academic learning to be happy and succeed in life.

Helping Children Form Healthy Relationships

Sam is six years old and the youngest of three children. He is a bright, intuitive child who has no trouble with his work in school. On the playground, however, Sam cannot relate to other children. He does not engage in any form of social play. He bullies most of the children, and thus, none of them want to be his friend. Upon questioning his parents, I found out Sam bullied the entire family at home. He controlled where the family sat, which programs they watched, and even what food they ate. Sam had total control of his environment. If this was challenged or threatened, he threw tantrums to get his way.

Successful relationships are based on the acceptance of another person. It also involves effective communication and a well-developed sense of the other person's need.

A good relationship balances the ability to concede

with the ability to be assertive without wanting to dominate.

The process of building healthy relationships begins at home. In the busy daily routine of parenting, it is often difficult for parents to find the time to be with their child. As parents, we are the main relationship teachers. Our family grouping is the model which teaches our children how to relate. The way we communicate with our children influences how our relationship with them develops and how effectively they can form and maintain relationships in later life. The way family members relate to each other also plays a vital role in determining the effectiveness of the child's relationships.

The language and vocabulary of healthy relationships is open, soft, and accepting rather than closed, harsh, and demanding. "Could you" is better than "Do this now." "I would like you to" is better than "If you don't, I will." The language we use and the other ways we communicate with our children and listen to them tell them a lot about how they can deal with others. If we hug our kids, laugh with them, cry with them, and are open with our feelings, then our children will do likewise.

In teaching children about relationships and in passing on to them the skills for forming and developing relationships, it is also essential to help them understand the value of personal space. By being comfortable when the child wants to be left alone and not always wanting to know what the child is doing or thinking, we send the message it is okay to have personal space.

As the facilitators of the child's ability to relate,

it is how we relate to each other

and other adults who are a part of our child's world

that influences the child the most.

We must always teach our children to be tolerant of other's differences. This difference may be related to something as simple as the color of hair or maybe in the form of a physical handicap or disability. Difference can also be in the form of ability, where a child who is bright and quick with his work needs to be understanding and accepting of others who are slower.

Trust is an essential foundation for relationships. When we show children, we believe in what they are saying, we give them the message that they are credible and trustworthy, and we help them have an equal and open relationship with others.

Our children's relationships are based on what they experience.

Whatever we as parents bring into our relationship with our kids will directly influence our children's behavior and their ability to form and maintain meaningful relationships throughout their lives. We must invest in our relationship with our children to ensure that our children fit acceptably into society!

Peer Problems

From the time children enter school, peers take upon an increasingly meaningful and influential role in their lives. Peers become key providers of support, companionship, advice, and affirmation as the child progresses through the elementary school years and adolescence. As children mature, parents provide these essential functions less, thus becoming less involved in their child's day-to-day activities.

Although the early school years are important for socialization and the development of social skills, third to fifth grades present a pivotal time during which peer relations become increasingly meaningful, and children become ever more concerned about their social acceptance. Social dynamics stabilize, and cliques emerge. During this time that children also become more independent and strive to establish a separate identity from that of their parents.

Experiencing peer problems at this time can have an exceptionally long-lasting impact. If children see themselves as socially incompetent, victimized, or rejected, these negative self-views may take hold and serve to accentuate peer problems. These problems typically fall within two broad categories: bullying/victimization and rejection.

Bullying and Victimization: When we think of bullying, we typically think of physical assaults, such as hitting, kicking, shoving, or hurting in some physical manner, and direct verbal assaults, such as teasing and insulting. Another form of bullying includes stealing from others.

The goal of bullying is to control, intimidate, and humiliate another person. Experiencing bullying is extremely damaging and places children at significant risk for adjustment problems.

Additionally, when victims feel hurt or are pushed to the limit, they may act out, becoming aggressive toward those bullying them. Unfortunately, their ineffective attempts to confront a bullying situation may serve to provoke more aggression.

What can parents do to prevent their children from getting bullied?

If a child is physically abusing your child, tell him always to walk or play with friends, not alone. Make a list with your child as to where he can go and places to get help. If your child is a victim, he needs to know that he is not the one with the problem.

Have your child tell the school guidance counselor the name of the bully who is victimizing him. Or you might try talking to the principal or his teachers directly.

Bullies like to show off by embarrassing someone in front of a group of people. They might not be so tough without a crowd. If verbal abuse is the problem, tell your child to be firm, try to stick up for himself, and tell the bully, "I don't like what you're doing to me, and I want you to stop."

If the child is old enough to reason, have him tell the bully how it feels to be bullied. Do not stress what the bully did since the accusations might make him defensive and be less likely to listen. If he is willing to listen, he might be ready to change. However, if he is unwilling to listen and starts getting nasty, your child is better off staying away from him or ignoring him. If the verbal abuse turns into threats, ask your child to notify someone in authority immediately.

Having his things stolen victimizes and violates a child. Put your child's name on everything that belongs to him. It also helps not to allow him to take items of any significant importance or value in school. If the child's things are still taken, have the bully reported.

Peer Rejection: Peer rejection involves the active dislike and avoidance of a child by many peers. Peers avoid playing or working with this child. They do not want to sit with the child at lunch and do not invite him to play. This child is avoided and excluded from participating in groups. Rejected children may maintain friendships with a small subset of children, sometimes also rejected, or they may be more socially isolated.

There are many different reasons why children are rejected by their peers. They may not cooperate or be responsive to others, or they may not know how to respond in certain social situations. Teaching a child the missing skills is often more effective in improving peer relationships than reducing negative behavior.

Many rejected children lack positive interaction skills, such as being cooperative, helpful, or considerate toward others. This suggests it is possible to help these children by teaching them positive ways to interact with others.

Peer relationships are essential to children's development. Friends not only provide companionship and relationship but meet other needs as well. Through interactions with peers, children learn valuable social skills. They learn how to do things like join groups, make new friends, participate in group problem solving, and manage competition and conflict. Thus, it is worth spending the time and effort in ensuring that your child shares a healthy and happy relationship with his peers!

Undesirable Friends

"Of late, Janet has started behaving very odd. She does not care about any of the family values and dresses distastefully. She is only nine and already wants to wear make-up! She has fallen behind in her studies and is always on the phone. It is all because of Samantha's influences on her. Janet was never like that before she became friends with Samantha," complains Tracy about her daughter Janet.

It is said that man is a social animal. To survive in our society, we must reach out and develop an association with people outside of our family. Once a child is seven or eight years of age, peers become influential in a child's life. A child's friendships have a unique place in her life and are different from the relationship shared with parents or siblings. As children become teenagers, most of them will gravitate towards their peers even if they are being rejected by their parents.

The effects of friendships in our children's lives can be seen in minor areas like fashion and hairstyles to more crucial issues like smoking, drinking, and romantic relationships among teenagers. Most teenagers take that first drink not because they are interested in the activity per se, but because their friends are doing it.

Our children's choice of friends is vital in determining who they become. Some friendships affect our children negatively. The importance of making sure our children cultivate the right friendships cannot be underestimated. How do you as a parent ensure that your child is not associating with undesirable friends who are leading your child down a self-destructive path or influencing her in the wrong way?

The mistake most parents make in dealing with their children's peers is making negative comments about them. Parents warn their children to stay away from certain friends and not have anything to do with them. When parents forbid something, they increase its appeal. When a parent makes negative comments about a child's friend, the child usually feels the need to become defensive. This strengthens the bond between the children. Thus, instead of breaking off the relationship, it usually reinforces it.

The best way to deal with undesirable friends is not to try to stop it,

but rather to try to control how it occurs.

Begin by inviting your child's friend to your home a few times. Then raise questions such as: "Do you think Tina acts responsibly?" or "Do you think Jane is considerate of others?" If not asked too often, questions like these give children the opportunity to realize that some of their friends may have undesirable qualities. They begin to view their friends differently and may soon become disillusioned and end the relationship.

Another way to eliminate your children's association with undesirable friends is to involve them in activities that keep them busy and cut down on the amount of time they have to be with these friends. Children have their special interests or hobbies, which can help keep them involved. Parents must encourage children to devote more time to these pursuits.

Inviting desirable youngsters to participate in family events is also helpful. This will allow your child to get to know other kids and make some meaningful and pleasant friendships. A wise philosopher once said, "Be slow in choosing your friends; it will help save you a lifetime of regret." All parents would like their children to be sociable, but not at the cost of breaking family rules or compromising family values.

Friendships give children the opportunity to share everyday experiences and interests and help define who they are. Thus, parents must make an extra effort in ensuring that their child's friends are right for them and the family!

Going to School for the First Time

There is a lot of excitement at home since little Jason is going to school for the first time. Mom and dad are ecstatic about Jason's future. Shopping for a school bag, uniform, books, and stationery has been a lot of fun. However, little Jason has no idea what he is getting into and what to expect of his day in this strange environment. He puts on his bag pack and uniform and is all set for this new adventure of his life, only to break out into uncontrollable sobs, complaints of nausea, and the desperate want to be with his mother. The school calls home and lets mom know about little Jason's crisis. She comes in very quickly to take her little darling home.

That is not how everyone who had been planning for this day had imagined it would turn out. Going to school for the first time can be a very scary experience for children. Parents need to take steps to make sure their little darlings are ready and set for the big day.

Some points to keep in mind when preparing your child to go to school for the first time:

1. **Talk to your child about all the pleasant experiences you had in school.** Tell him about the friends he will make and all the fun activities he will get to do. Show him pictures and videos of the new school. If possible, take him on a school tour before it starts and spend some time getting acquainted with the new surroundings. If possible, interact with his new teacher, so he builds a bond with her, thus feeling more comfortable.

2. **Make sure your child has some supervised time away from you before he starts school.** This could include a playschool or spending a night at grandmas. This helps build a sense of independence in the child, which is vital for his success in school.

3. **Prepare your child by talking about how the first day can be stressful and come up with ways of coping.** Take him through all the possible activities they might do with him on the first day to be more prepared.

4. **Go shopping for school supplies together.** A Barbie bag or a Scooby-doo water bottle can work as huge incentives.

5. **Rehearse the morning routine so that it is not stressful on the first day.** Practice waking up, eating breakfast, and getting ready. Once your child is familiar with the routine, he will be more comfortable on the first day.

6. **Do not panic if your child sheds a few tears when he sees you leave.** He will probably stop after you leave. If your child is screaming and howling, leave as quickly as possible, and most likely, he will calm down in a few minutes.

7. **Sometimes, it helps to sit with your child a little every day, weaning him off slowly.** However, this is only possible if the school authorities allow it.

Parents play a significant role in preparing their little ones for the long-awaited first day of school. Taking the proper steps to ensure a comfortable transition will result in less anxiety for both parent and child.

Children experience anxiety not only when going to school for the first time but also when going back to school after a long, relaxing summer break. Here are some ways parents can prepare their kids to have a healthy transition to school after a blissful holiday (well, at least that is how the kids feel).

- Make sure your child is prepared with all the supplies he needs. Also, ensure all their holiday homework is done so that he feels better prepared for school.
- To get a good start, your child needs to get enough sleep and have a healthy breakfast. You can start putting your kids early to bed and wake them up early a few days before school starts, to help in this transition.
- It is natural for your kids to feel anxious about the first day in school after their break; talk to them about all the fun things that school offers, such as meeting friends, buying new school supplies, and making some new friends. It is also essential to discuss with your kids any concerns that they might have about going back to school and offer your support.
- You can motivate your child by offering reinforcers like a great family outing during the weekend so that your child has something to look forward to after a stressful transitional week at school.
- If possible, drive your child to school on the first day to aid with the feeling of comfort and familiarity.

I am sure you all remember experiencing mixed emotions when going back to school yourself. It is always helpful for parents to be one step ahead in being prepared to avoid being caught off guard. Parents must offer support, encouragement, and guidance to see kids through this transition successfully!

Helping Children Adjust to a New School

Your family's move can be an exciting time for your children, and you or it can be a stressful and sad time. One of the most challenging aspects of moving for children is the adjustment to a new school. Your child may have distressing feelings about going to a new school, sad about leaving old friends, or angry with you about moving. Whether your child is making a mid-year move to a new city, taking the leap from elementary to middle school, or advancing to high school, the first few weeks are filled with anxiety as well as excitement.

The following tips will help your child make a smooth transition to a new school.

1. **Make it a team effort.** If you are choosing among a few schools, talk with your children about what each school has to offer. When it comes time to select specific classes, make sure they are a part of the process.

2. **Keep a positive focus.** As the first day draws near, begin talking to your children about their expectations, hopes, and fears for the upcoming

school year. Reassure them that other children have the same feelings and that it is normal to be a little anxious. Offer school as a place where they will learn new things and make friends.

3. **Encourage school involvement by your children.** It is important to encourage participation in one or two activities that particularly interest them. Children are more likely to be engaged academically if they feel connected through a school activity, club, or sport. Talk to them about their goals for the year and how they might be involved in school outside the classroom.

4. **Early to bed, Early to rise.** If your children have enjoyed a vacation of late nights and lazy mornings, getting them up for school on the first day can be difficult. Help make this transition easier by starting their school-year sleep routine at least a week in advance.

5. **Take a trial run.** Take some time before the start of school to make sure you and your children know what to do and where to go on that first morning. Show your children where the bus stop is, or if they walk, show them the safest route to the school, avoiding routes with vacant lots and places where there are not many people. Warn your children to always walk with a friend and scout out safe houses in case of emergency. If you can find out what classrooms your children will be in, visit the classrooms ahead of time, so they know exactly where to go in the morning. You may even want to call up the school to find out about any special first-day procedures.

6. **Stock up on supplies.** On or before the first day of school, find out what materials your children need. Most schools provide a handy list for the younger grades, but if not, take it upon yourself to ask and purchase them as soon as possible. Middle and high school students should be sure to take along a notebook and a writing instrument with them.

7. **Prepare the night before to avoid the early morning rush; organize what you can the night before.** Lay out clothes, make a snack, and assemble any supplies your child needs. Be sure to get everyone up extra early so you will have enough time to get ready calmly and get out the door on time.

8. **Get a healthy start.** Encourage your children to eat a good breakfast. Pack a healthy snack to help them get through the day.

9. **Accompany your little one.** Even if your elementary school children will be regularly riding the bus or walking to school, you may want to take them yourself on the first day, particularly if they seem nervous.

10. **Introduce yourself.** Young children are often shy with a new teacher. If you take your children to school on the first day, you might want to go into the classroom and introduce your children to their teachers. Let the teacher know about any special interests or challenges your child has.

Transitions are exciting opportunities for children to learn and grow.

Parents play an essential role in making children feel comfortable as they move to new educational settings. Families often benefit from a move, regardless of its reason, but it is up to the parents to help their children see the benefit. With kind words and encouragement, children will love the move, their new home, and their new school just as they did the old one.

Do You Go to School with Your Child?

One of the most complex relationships we can have is with the school our child attends. Most parents understand the importance of being actively involved in their child's education. Parents and the school authorities need to work together to ensure the success of the child. However, some parents find it difficult to become involved with their child's school.

A good relationship with your child's teacher is essential for you to nurture and educate your child. There are several ways to ensure that you are a positive force in your child's education. Get to know your child's school by planning a visit. During your visit, look around the school, talk to the principal and your child's teachers. Find out what your child's school mission statement is, how they plan to accomplish those goals, and what problems they encounter. Make it clear that as a parent, you would like to be an integral part of your child's education, which means that the school's well-being is of interest to you.

Communicate with your child's teachers. You do not have to wait for an open house at the school to meet your child's teachers. Go ahead and schedule a meeting to discuss any concerns. These meetings are a two-way street. Just as you are there to learn more about how your child is performing in the school setting, teachers are interested in learning about any issues at home that may be affecting the child's school performance. You can also periodically call or email your child's teachers throughout the school year to determine how your child is performing.

Find out whether your children are:

- Completing their in-class work, homework, and projects

- Studying for quizzes and tests

- Performing well

- Working to their potential

- Developing the competencies and skills necessary to demonstrate academic achievement

Work with your children at home. No matter how well they are doing in school, children still benefit from your advice and participation at home. Many schools require planners or agendas of some sort for students to write down all homework assignments, upcoming tests, and projects. Check your child's planner regularly to see whether your child has homework. You could also use the planner to convey messages to your child's teachers and receive information from them.

Attend Open Houses and Parent-Teacher Conferences. Far from one more burdening activity in an already over-scheduled life, Open Houses can provide a wealth of information to the parents. This is an excellent opportunity for parents to meet their children's class teachers and the school counselor, principal, and other staff. You will get valuable insight into your child's performance from all parties concerned. At Open Houses, you will get a chance to follow your child's schedule by going to all their classes, allowing for an ideal opportunity to meet all your child's teachers. The purpose of the school conference is to find out how well your child is doing, what her strengths and weaknesses are, and what you can do to help your child learn effectively.

Become and stay active in your child's school. You can volunteer to help on field trips and school concerts. This will provide you further inroads into becoming more actively involved with your child's education. If you have the time or unique talents, volunteering can be an excellent way to show your children you are deeply involved in their school lives.

Active parenting takes time, but the time you spend helping your children become personally and academically successful will return benefits to you tenfold. Your positive involvement and time are directly proportionate to helping students of today become successful adults tomorrow.

The Socially Anxious Kid

Why are some kids so comfortable in social situations while others struggle and barely manage to get a word out of their mouth in similar environments? Over the past few weeks, I have had at least three parents ask me about their "socially anxious child." They were concerned about what was causing the anxiety and what they could do to help. To be able to help, we must first understand the problem.

Social Anxiety can be very debilitating.

It can prevent people from achieving the levels of success

that is achieved by those who are outgoing.

Social Anxiety has several suspected causes. Research has shown that anxiety has a genetic component, which means some children are born with an anxious temperament. Babies who are emotionally sensitive and easily intimidated are more likely to grow up to be fearful children. Anxious parents may have children who are anxious too. Inconsistent caregiving and not feeling attached to their parents may cause some children to be anxious. Over-protective parenting may result in children being inhibited and afraid, especially of new situations.

Also, children who have been isolated from others for the first few years of their lives may lack the necessary social skills that enable easy interaction with unfamiliar people. Children who are teased or bullied by significant people in their lives (parents, siblings, and other close family members or friends) may tend to be anxious. Finally, the fear of failure in children who have been pushed too many times beyond their capabilities and then made to feel bad when they did not "measure up" may manifest itself as social anxiety.

Socially anxious children have an excessive worry about what others think about them. They are always worried about saying or doing something embarrassing. They avoid large gatherings, new social situations and are extremely uncomfortable when someone focuses on them.

As parents, we have a natural tendency to try and protect our children from pain or from things that frighten them. However, protecting an anxious child from the things he fears can result in reinforcing the fear. The first thing we must do for the anxious child is stop protecting him from public life. The reality is that we all must deal with people.

Certain points should be kept in mind when trying to help your fearful child. First, do not label your child. Children tend to live up to the labels given to them. Also, never criticize or mock your child. Your child needs extra comforting and support along with reminders about his skills and successes to overcome anxiety.

Building their self-esteem is probably one of the most essential ingredients

to help children cope with social anxiety.

Talk to your child about times when you felt anxious in social situations and how you coped with it. Ask your child to talk about his fears and then try to come up with a coping strategy. Praise outgoing behavior in your child. Commend your child when an unfamiliar situation is handled well, or a new person is greeted and spoken with. Aim for small, incremental steps and praise your child for the progress. For example, saying "hello" to another child may be a big first step.

Role-play with your child so that he is better prepared to face new situations. Create situations like inviting your child's friend to visit to provide an opportunity for social interaction for your child. Talk to your child about the benefits of outgoing behavior, like having more friends and enjoying activities more. Lastly, model the desired outgoing behavior. Children learn behaviors best what they see adults displaying the same. If you feel that you need additional support in dealing with this problem, contact your child's teacher or counselor for some social skills training and relaxation techniques.

Help your child overcome social anxiety by providing your comfort, love, support, and encouragement. Also, try to keep reinforcing and finding successes in what your child does. Confidence is what is needed here.

Recognized success will help the child achieve that confidence!

Listen to Your Boy's Silence

Consider these statistics:

- Boys are four times more likely to commit suicide.
- Boys are three times more likely than girls to be victims of violence.
- Male students have lower educational aspirations.
- Boys are fifty percent more likely to be held back a grade than girls.
- Boys are substantially more likely to endure disciplinary problems, be suspended from classes, or drop out of school entirely.

For a long time, it has been girls and their issues that get attention. Now, it has become more critical than ever to focus on the emotions and feelings of boys. It is easy to deal with girl's emotions since they are more vocal about their feelings and express them in ways that make it easy to provide the needed support. However, since boys have a different and more indirect way of dealing with emotions, it is easy to neglect their needs.

In our society, people have certain expectations about how boys should process and express emotions. From the time he is old enough to understand, a boy is taught to "behave like a man." If he is hurt, he is told not to cry, for that is what girls do. He is praised for being strong, for enduring pain without whimpering, for being brave. Boys are often discouraged from displaying "soft" emotions like tenderness, lest their friends ridicule them. Understanding boy's behaviors will empower us to help them deal with emotions effectively.

Some methods boys use to process their feelings include slamming doors, burying themselves in some activity like playing a videogame or exercising, going into their cave to be left alone, and problem-solving. This is different from the techniques girls use to deal with their feelings, which usually include crying and talking to someone. Because of their indirect nature, it is sometimes easy to overlook boys' behaviors as signs of trouble. By appreciating the structural differences between males and females, we can understand boys while helping them manage their sentiments.

We must create safety zones for boys by understanding and recognizing

their emotional needs and creating an inviting and caring environment for them.

The following are some suggestions of how to help boys who are troubled be open with their feelings:

- **Pay attention to the mantra "everything is fine."** This is a common and simply said phrase that is often used to mask the symptoms of more serious issues such as depression. Look beyond angry, aggressive, or unruly behavior for genuine concerns.

- **Learn new ways to talk to boys so they do not feel afraid or ashamed to share their true feelings**. Avoid using shaming language and forming a judgment about situations under discussion. Ask "how" and "what" questions, which encourage boys to be open.

- **Accept their emotional schedules**. Remember, boys who do share their feelings often take longer to do so than girls do.

- **Connect through action.** Often, simply engaging in physical activity with boys enables them to be open.

- **Help boys take off their masks by telling them stories about your experiences.** Share times you were challenged, scared, embarrassed, disappointed, or felt deep emotional turmoil.

- **Give boys undivided attention daily.** Let them know that you are eager to know what is happening in their world.

- **Encourage the expression of a full range of emotions.** Boys need to know all feelings are valid.

- **When boys express vulnerable feelings, avoid teasing or taunting them.** Instead of teasing, mirror back in an empathetic way the feelings you sense they are trying to convey. Let boys know they do not need to be "sturdy oaks." It is okay to cry and ask for help.

- **Create a model of masculinity that is broad and inclusive.** Help them realize that there is no single way of being male.

There are important differences in the way boys and girls express their feelings. We need to help our boys grow up to be well-socialized, emotionally regulated, decent men, and it is up to parents and other adults to ensure that happens.

Understanding Your Child's Temperament

A mother attending my workshop said, "one of my kids is so different from the other two. I feel like someone dropped a bird from a different family into my nest." It is not uncommon to feel this way when one of your children is vastly different from the other. Some children are quiet, focused, and sensitive, while others are active, distractible, and get into trouble a lot. So, what accounts for these differences in children?

Children are born with a temperament that is their natural style of interacting with or reacting to people, places, and things. The realization that many behavioral tendencies are inborn and not the result of bad parenting is perhaps one of the most critical insights parents gain from learning more about temperament. By understanding the patterns of temperament, parents can adapt their parenting approach in areas such as expectations, encouragement, and discipline to suit the child's individual needs.

According to some studies, there are three basic temperaments: Easy or Flexible, Difficult and Active, and Slow to warm up or Cautious.

Easy or flexible children are mostly cool and content; they are regular in sleeping and eating habits, are adaptable, more relaxed, and do not get easily upset. Difficult and active children are often picky, irregular in feeding and sleeping habits, scared of new people and situations, get easily disturbed by noise and commotion, are high strung, more active, and have strong reactions. Slow to warm up or cautious children are relatively inactive and fussy, they tend to withdraw or react negatively to new situations, but their reactions gradually become more affirmative with continuous exposure.

A parent who came to see me said, "A few months ago, my husband and I had to go out of town for a few days, so my parents came to the house to stay with my two daughters. Even though one of my daughters adores her grandparents, she had an exceedingly difficult time with the change. She cried frequently, was easily upset, and was very unhappy the entire time. On the other hand, daughter number two was perfectly content and hardly seemed to notice we were gone."

As parents, you need to understand your child's temperamental traits and tailor your parenting style accordingly. Respect the child's uniqueness and do not compare him to others. Listen to and understand your child's point of view. Set limits to help your child develop self-control. Regard their opinions but remain firm on essential boundaries. Be a good role model because children learn by imitation.

Also, be aware of your temperament and adjust your natural responses when they clash with your child's responses. If you are an "active" parent with a "quiet" child, your child's dawdling and daydreaming probably stress you. Conversely, if you are a "quiet" parent with an "active" child, you are probably drained by your child's constant activity. Identifying this difference enables you to handle it better.

The match between the child's temperament and the demands or expectations of his or her environment significantly improve relationships.

Parents who are tuned into their child's temperament and recognize their child's strengths will find life more pleasant. Understanding that some of the kid's traits may be predispositions, they are born with can ease a whole lot of strain and may calm some of the more "temperamental" moments in family life!

Helping your child Build Tolerance

Being intolerant of others' differences is a double-edged sword. When children begin to perceive "different" as wrong or something to make fun of, they will also fear being different. For most school children, social acceptance is a priority, and the need to fit in and belong to a group is so vital that they are ready to sacrifice their individuality to achieve this. They tend to focus more on what is suitable for the world around them rather than for themselves.

Humans vary in terms of shape, size, color, and so on, and these differences make the world a colorful place to live in. It is essential to teach children to be tolerant and curious of these differences rather than judgmental and unaccepting.

It is time for parents to recognize the importance of teaching children to respect people of all sizes, shapes, colors, racial backgrounds, religions, and abilities. When children respect others, they also begin to value and appreciate their differences. All this helps to prepare our children to live peacefully in the diverse world in which they live.

Tolerance can be taught in very subtle ways. Parents can consider some of the following tips when teaching their children to respect diversity:

• Modeling healthy attitudes towards others is the first step towards teaching your children tolerance. Consistently demonstrate an attitude of respect for others.

• Children are very observant and often listen to any comments you make concerning those who are different. Resist making jokes or putting down those who are different, even if done with harmless intent.

• Pause and discuss with your children any biases portrayed in the media. Counter a disrespectful comment or behavior toward a group with a respectful and calm refutation. Talk about characters who treat and do not treat each other with respect and how their reactions could have been better.

• Monitor the shows your children are watching. Try to ensure they watch shows that send positive and healthy messages.

• Be honest and respectful in answering questions your child may have about those who are different.

• Teach children to acknowledge differences in the family, especially siblings. Show respect toward the individual differences in your children, thus helping them appreciate differences in others.

• Try to choose a school or extra-curricular activity in which your child can interact with children of diverse backgrounds. This will give your child an opportunity to interact with those who are different.

• Have fun learning about other cultures and traditions. Educate your children about the holidays and religious celebrations that are different from their own.

• Help your children acknowledge their strengths and feel good about their diversity. Teach your children to value and respect their differences.

Our children need to be taught to be tolerant of those who are different, not only in terms of cultural heritage but also those who are different in intellectual and physical abilities.

Key Points

> Building positive peer relations is probably one of the most important developmental tasks a child must accomplish.

> One strategy that works very well to help kids build social skills is "stop-think-act."

> Psychologists suggest that social and emotional development are equally important to academic learning to be happy and succeed in life.

> A good relationship balances the ability to concede with the ability to be assertive without wanting to dominate.

> As the facilitators of the child's ability to relate, it is how we relate to each other and other adults who are a part of our child's world that influences the child the most.

> Our children's relationships are based on what they experience.

> Transitions are exciting opportunities for children to learn and grow.

➤ Social Anxiety can be very debilitating. It can prevent people from achieving the levels of success that are achieved by those who are outgoing.

➤ Building their self-esteem is probably one of the most essential ingredients to help children cope with Social Anxiety.

➤ Recognized success will help the child achieve that confidence!

➤ We must create safety zones for boys by understanding and recognizing their emotional needs and creating an inviting and caring environment.

➤ Our children need to be taught to be tolerant of those who are different in terms of cultural heritage and those who are different in intellectual and physical abilities.

➤ Psychologists believe that all of us are born with a tendency toward certain temperaments. Temperaments predispose us to enjoy some activities more than others.

➤ The match between the child's temperament and the demands or expectations of his environment significantly improves relationships.

➤ The best way to deal with undesirable friends is not to try to stop it but rather to control how it occurs.

Section 3: All in the Family

Let's Bring the New Baby Home

I remember when my sister had just delivered her angelic baby girl. At the time, her older daughter was four years old, so naturally, the concern of how the older one would welcome and accept the new baby started a few days after the baby was conceived.

Many children welcome a younger sibling.

However, some of them can react adversely due to the insecurity they feel.

Children experience a mixture of positive and negative feelings. They feel envious and left out and at the same time feel proud and concerned about their younger siblings. My niece has been going through her cycle of feeling affectionate towards her little sister and other times feeling angry because her mommy does not spend as much time with her as she used to.

Children need assistance with making the transition from having the sole ownership of your time and attention to sharing it with someone else. Research has shown that between eighteen months and three years is probably the most challenging time for children to adjust to a new baby. Before eighteen months, children are too young to realize, and at the ages of four and above, children are more mature and better at handling insecurities. Thus, consider the timing when planning your new baby!

You can also start preparing your child by involving her in shopping for the baby and decorating the baby's room. When the baby comes, include your older child in caretaking. Involve her at bath and changing time. These simple acts will make your older child feel responsible and allow her to spend more time with you. Also, you can make feeding and changing rituals a time to sing songs together or tell stories.

Reading books to your children and talking to them about the realities of how much time and energy will be spent on taking care of the baby assists them with understanding the changes taking place. Acquaint them with the facts that the baby will probably not be a playmate for some time. Initially, the baby will be drinking and sleeping all the time.

Another subject that should be addressed and taught to the older child is handling the baby, which is often very rough, innately. Their way of showing affection can be very forceful on the baby. Parents must show the older child how to handle her sibling instead safely and gently of keeping her from playing with the baby, which will eventually build up resentment. You can also help your child practice the correct manner of handling the baby with a doll.

An often-understated possibility is some children regress when a new baby comes into a family. Some might indulge in attention-seeking behaviors, and others may have increased toilet accidents and sleep trouble. These behaviors will generally disappear in a couple of months as the child matures and can better handle her insecurities.

Catch your child displaying appropriate behavior towards her sibling. Praise her for the times she is gently stroking the baby or reading to him or her. There is nothing more powerful in teaching a behavior than praise. Also, make sure you identify and comment upon these behaviors when seen on TV or among other children.

Spend time every day with your older child. Even if it is twenty minutes of one-on-one time when the baby is sleeping, spend this time asking the older child about her school day and friends. The older child must not feel left out.

Once my younger niece arrived, suddenly, her older sister became regarded as old enough to be more independent and mature. My sister had to constantly remind herself that her older one is only four and still a child who is still dependent on her for several things.

Listen to your child when she is expressing herself. Acknowledge her insecurities and teach your child healthy ways of expressing the anger or jealousy she feels toward her little sibling. Discounting your child's feelings will make her feel invalidated. Your child needs to know it is ok for her to be mad or upset with the baby, but hurting the baby will not be accepted.

It is a stressful time for children when a new baby arrives. The very thought of sharing mom and dad with someone else can upset little children, and they may feel unloved, angry, and frustrated. Preparing your older child for having a new baby in the house and supporting her emotionally to deal with the adjustment will help you and your little one tremendously. Before you know it, your little darlings will be playing house together or scheming up ways of hiding their chocolates from your notice!

Families that Fight

Little Jasmine came to me one morning trembling with fear. When asked about what had made her so scared, the eight-year-old related the previous night's display of violent outbursts and explosive anger by her parents towards each other. Every couple will agree that marriage is no bed of roses and has its share of ups and downs. However, parents often forget that their aggressive acts and abusive behaviors affect them and their children.

Each day, countless kids arrive at school having witnessed such antisocial acts from family members. This has a significant effect on the child's behavior and performance. Children living in homes full of aggression often display **poor academic skills**. These kids are not tuned into the learning process. They are not motivated to learn because they have little hope for the future.

Also, children caught in a cycle of family anger **lack social skills** and develop **low self-esteem** and **depression**. These kids may regress to an earlier stage under stress and thus are **immature** and lack impulse control and empathy towards others' feelings. With no positive role models, these children are often unable to deal appropriately with their anger resulting in **aggressive acts and violence** towards peers.

Parents must learn to express their anger and frustration privately and in ways that do not hurt their children. Here are some pointers to keep in mind when the going gets rough:

- Learn to read anger signals and immediately engage in relaxation techniques like deep breathing or grounding exercises.
- When you are calm, try and figure out the real reason behind your frustrations. Are you feeling stressed, neglected, or tired? When you have figured the cause, try and deal with it healthily.
- Develop a conflict management plan. Explore the problematic situations and work together to generate possible solutions.
- When in a fight, avoid name-calling, threatening, and door slamming. Work on building effective communication skills.
- If you have issues to resolve with your spouse, wait until the kids are asleep and then do so.
- If you end up arguing in front of the children, make sure you explain to them later that you were upset and that it had nothing to do with them. Let them know that although daddy and mommy fought, it does not mean they do not love each other or them.
- Talk to the kids about how you may have said things you do not mean during your argument. Also, explain to your

children that the way you handled your anger was wrong and talk about more healthy habits.

- Children are very observant and sensitive. They pick up on tensions and undercurrents but are not particularly good at identifying the cause. When they hear raised voices and slammed doors, they cannot help but question, "Is it me?" let your children know that the fight was not their fault.

There is no doubt that children who are caught in the cycle of family anger are victims

and may present their family experiences in their school and other settings.

Your children's lives revolve around you, and they look to you for security and comfort. Rumbling fights between parents leave children feeling insecure and unsure. So, before you have the next raging battle with your spouse, pause for a moment and think of the effect it will have on your little angels!

Fights Between Siblings

You are home after a long day at work. You are tired and hungry, and it is time to fix supper for the kids who are at each other's throats, fighting about who gets to control the TV remote. You had hoped that your kids would have learned to resolve issues peacefully by this age, but at ages ten and fourteen, they are fighting more than ever. You wonder, will this fighting ever stop!

The purpose of fights is usually to gain a parent's attention and support,

or to show superiority and power over one another.

Regardless of the purpose behind a fight, verbal and physical fighting between siblings is nerve-wracking to parents. Parents want their children to get along, and conflict can upset the entire household. If you have tried different methods to get your children to stop fighting and none of them have worked, you might want to consider *not opposing* the behavior. This may sound ridiculous, but it may be just what is needed to change your home from being a battleground to being a peaceful place to live.

One way of handling fighting is to tell children, "If you want to fight, you have to go outside." Once outside, the fighting seldom continues. Since the purpose of most fights is to gain a parent's attention, when the parents are no longer in sight, the argument stops automatically. If one child is weaker than another, that child will probably not put himself into this situation since there is no hope of rescue. However, parents must know when to step in. You must step in either when the fight repeatedly happens about the same concern. Also, when the fight can injure any or both parties involved, it is time for a parent to step in and protect the children.

If desired, parents can set aside fifteen minutes each day when their children are permitted to fight. Tell the children that this is the only time of the day when they can fight. If they begin fighting before the designated time, remind them of the rule. When the time for a fight arrives, bring the children together and tell them this is the time to fight. This technique is nearly always effective in eliminating any desire the children may have had to fight. When fights are structured, they lose their appeal.

One crucial point to bear in mind is that parents should resist taking sides when their children fight. To achieve harmony, follow the rule that everyone involved in the fight gets the same punishment. Unless a parent is 100 percent certain that the fight is the fault of one child, treat all in the same way.

Parents should also make sure that they do not compare siblings with each other. This almost always intensifies jealousy and envy, which can take the form of physical or verbal fights among siblings.

Spend time teaching your children healthy ways to resolve conflicts.

Future generations will need the skills of negotiation and cooperation in their personal and professional lives. Parents can make an incredible difference in their children's lives by teaching these skills to them early!

Remember that when you help your children get along better, you are preparing them for significant relationships in the future with their friends, colleagues, spouses, and their children.

Working Parents Trials and Tribulations

I was conducting a workshop on parenting teens when a very distressed mother came up to me and started to share her story.

"My husband and I are both working parents and have to work long hours to provide for our children." With a slight beam in her eyes, she began telling me about her kids, "I have two children, Stacy, who is thirteen, and Jack, who is ten. They are so talented and bright."

Suddenly, the beam was replaced by sadness when she continued, "But they do not realize this and spend most of their time watching television or on the phone with their friends. They do not listen, are very mean to me, and probably hate me for not spending time with them. They do not understand that I have no choice! They fear their father and tend to behave when he is around, but his schedule does not allow for much interaction with the kids. I am also tired by the end of the day and have no

65

patience to deal with their tantrums and tend to give in a lot. I know this is wrong. Please help me!" She then started to cry bitterly.

Socioeconomic conditions force several parents to work long hours, thus compelling them to leave their little darlings in the care of a babysitter or, when that is unaffordable, alone at home.

Ideally, children should be supervised by an adult in all settings. However, many times this is not possible, and children find themselves home alone without adult supervision.

How can parents deal with ensuring the healthy development of their children even when they are not around?

There are a few things that parents can do to ensure that each child is developing in ways that are healthy and beneficial:

- When both parents work, it is essential that you individually spend some special time with the children. Each parent must plan at least twenty minutes every day with each child, giving the child their complete attention. This is the time to talk about your child's day's happenings, play games, and plan for activities that you can do together.
- Parents need to set rules and routines that are to be followed by all the family members. These help children feel that they are being supervised even when the parents are away. Appropriate consequences for not following the rules and rewards for doing so also need to be discussed and set so that children are aware of what

those are. Working parents often fail to discipline their children because they experience a certain amount of guilt about not spending time with them. You need to bear in mind that not spending time is no excuse to indulge the children.

- CONSISTENCY...CONSISTENCY...CONSISTENCY! This aspect cannot be stressed enough. Often, parents set rules; however, they fail to follow through with the consequences or rewards since they are tired after a long day of work. Only when children know you mean business will they follow through with your instructions.

- If your children are alone at home, make sure they are aware of the safety rules. Tell your children not to answer the door unless he or she knows who is there. Give your children all the emergency numbers they can contact in an unforeseen event. Also, do not allow your children to have their friends over when they are alone.

- If you choose to employ a babysitter, check out the person's references. Talk to your children about appropriate and inappropriate behavior on the part of the sitter and how they must immediately report the latter. In case you are considering daycare for your children, check out the facility. Spend a few hours observing the place and talk to other parents who use the same daycare.

- Visit your child's school regularly to stay in touch with his teachers and be informed about any difficulties that your child may be experiencing. Also, make sure you try to attend as many school extra-curricular events, parent-teacher conferences, and back-to-school nights as possible so that your child feels that you are involved in his academic life. Parental involvement is vital for a child's success at school.

- Make the most of weekends. Plan family activities and outings that will help you connect with your children.

Ideally, it would be great to have at least one parent around all the time, but this is not always possible. Do not feel guilty if you are a working parent. It is the many little things you do with your child like making popcorn, playing games, and watching movies they will remember!

Children of Divorce

Divorce is an unpleasant situation. It is one of the most traumatic and devastating events to endure. Parents are as emotionally wounded as children. The family unit is the most significant critical stability for young children. Parents give love, provide emotional support, teach their children skills, and educate them about life, as well as serve as role models. The breakup of the family unit through a divorce can be a heart-wrenching experience for children.

Divorce can adversely affect a child in terms of

their behavior, school, relationships, and self-esteem.

Every child experiences a range of emotions during the process of her parent's divorce. Children experience feelings like grief, sadness, anger, guilt, and confusion. Parents need to make sure their children's emotions are validated and dealt with healthily. You must acknowledge your children are upset that you are getting a divorce and that they are in distress. You can let them know that it is ok to talk to you about it. Even if they feel furious at you, assure them you will still listen to them. You can also offer to have them talk to other people, including school counselors, social workers, therapists, and other professionals.

Since children are the ones most intricately connected to the ex-spouse, it is easy to vent negative feelings against the other parent to them. However, this behavior almost always backfires and may result in alienating your child from you. If you cannot say anything good about your ex-partner, do not say anything.

Divorce can throw the child's entire life into a whirlwind.

There will more than likely be financial instabilities due to loss in income of the parent who has moved out. There may be a change in residence or schools. Also, for both parents and children, holidays and birthdays after a divorce can be some of the most challenging events to deal with, traumatic even. As many things as possible in the children's lives must remain the same. Familiarity with as many things as possible, with the least amount of disruption, is crucial to minimizing the emotional damage divorce causes to the children. It is also essential that the parent living away is still actively involved in the child's life. The ideal relationship for children of divorce with the parent who has moved out is to have them close by and there when the child wants or needs them. Both parents should be at all important events in a child's life, including parent/teacher conferences, ball games, plays, dance recitals, and proms.

Some other things to keep in mind are that a child amidst a divorce situation needs to be reassured that she is loved. She needs to know that she will be taken care of and will still have a home. The child also needs to be told repeatedly that the divorce is between mom and dad. Often, children feel that the divorce is their fault or that the parent is leaving because they do not want to be with the child anymore. Children must be told and made to understand this is **not** true. Do not assume that your child knows this.

Children handle divorce most successfully when parents work together for the children's sake. It is critical for the children's well-being that both parents continue to play essential roles in their lives. The most important thing for you to remember is that even though divorce may be difficult on you, you owe it to your child to minimize its effects upon her life.

Children Who Hurt Themselves

Dear Ms. Rachna,

I have a secret that I haven't shared with anyone. Often when I feel really anxious or stressed, I cut myself with a blade. I have so many cut marks all over my arms and legs that I have run out of space. I am seventeen years old and have been doing this since I was fourteen. I know this is probably not right, but I cannot stop myself. Sometimes, the emotions I feel are so overwhelming that hurting myself is the only thing that makes me feel better. Please help. - Cutter

An increasing number of children, especially teenagers, are resorting to hurting themselves in a desperate attempt to deal with the emotional dysregulation they experience. Eleventh-graders Margaret and Sheila are best friends. They came to see me one day and showed me the cuts on their hands they had made to deal with their stresses. For Margaret, it was an attempt to deal with the excruciating emotional pain of getting over a breakup. Simultaneously, for Sheila, it was a way of coping with the constant battles at home with parents who she felt did not understand her.

Self-injury can take the form of cutting, burning, pulling out hair, among others, and is more common among girls. Children hurt themselves as a means of coping with emotional turmoil. Cutting is also a desperate attempt to feel in control.

Children often feel like no one understands them

and thus, harm themselves to deal with the sense of emptiness they experience.

Children who are physically or sexually abused also tend to be cutters. They try to block out the terrible pain experienced because of these traumatic experiences by hurting themselves. Also, children who have other mental health problems like depression, anxiety, and eating disorders, are seen to hurt themselves because they have a more challenging time controlling impulses.

Sometimes, like all other things, teens tend to see cutting as a cool thing to do. Tina decided to try cutting herself because some of the girls in her school were doing it, and they advised her it was a great way to deal with the hurt she was experiencing due to her breakup. In one of our sessions, Tina claimed, "At first, it did not seem like a bad thing to do. After all, I wasn't hurting anyone else. And it did help me block out the pain I was dealing with. But I guess a part of me knew the harm I was causing myself and tried to stop. But it's hard!"

Children do not foresee that cutting or other self-injurious behavior can lead to infections, severe bruises, and in extreme cases, hospitalization or death.

Children fail to realize that cutting is only a temporary relief from the emotional pain they are experiencing.

Sometimes, self-injurious behavior becomes habit-forming, and children find it difficult to resist the urge to hurt themselves in stressful situations. The compulsion to engage in this dangerous behavior tends to take control over them.

Self-injurious behavior is confusing for both the child engaging in it and the parent. Thus, you need to educate yourself to understand the behavior better to be in a better position to help.

It never helps to lecture, reject, yell at, or emotionally plead with a child who cuts. Parents need to be patient with children who hurt themselves. If you know your child is engaging in self-injurious behaviors, you must communicate with your child about identifying the possible causes of this behavior like pressures to be perfect, broken relationships, loss, or trauma. You cannot stop a behavior without replacing it with a healthier one like exercising, writing a journal, or talking with a trusted adult.

It takes time for children to stop engaging in self-harm. Thus, you must be prepared for small steps in this direction. Do not shy away from seeking professional help for your child if you know she is engaging in this risky habit. There are mental health professionals who specialize in helping children with self-injurious tendencies.

It is natural to feel angry, hurt, and upset if you know the child whom you love so dearly is harming herself. However, the most important form of help you can offer your child is that of understanding and acceptance. You must believe they are not doing this to hurt you in any way but are troubled themselves in coping with the demands of the overly complex life they lead. Our children count on us for support and compassion to deal with the challenges they face.

Child Sexual Abuse

The number of children who are victims of sexual abuse each year is alarming. Yet, this subject is touched upon so little. One of my worst nightmares as a counselor is to see the face of a toddler who has been subjected to sexual abuse by a family member or friend. The long-term emotional and psychological damage that sexual abuse causes can be crushing for a child. Victims of sexual abuse have problems trusting others and forming meaningful relationships in their lives. They also start viewing themselves in a negative light.

Child sexual abuse can occur within the family, by a parent, stepparent, sibling, or another relative. It can be outside the home by a friend, neighbor, childcare provider, teacher, or stranger. No parent can be with a child every second of every day. However, the child can be taught to report when there is trouble so that something can be done to stop the harm. Children of all ages can be victims of abuse. Thus, the sooner we can prepare our children to deal with the situation, the better.

Sometimes, the child has a strong attachment to the predator and may find it difficult to report abuse incidents. Also, there are times when the predator may threaten the child if the child tries to break away from the sexual relationship. When sexual abuse occurs within the family, the child may fear the anger, jealousy, or shame of other family members or be afraid the family will break up if the secret is told. In these circumstances, parents need to be extra vigilant about the signs of abuse, including:

- Unusual interest in or avoidance of all things of a sexual nature
- Sleep problems or nightmares
- Depression or withdrawal from friends or family
- Seductiveness
- Statements that their bodies are dirty or damaged, or fear that there is something wrong with them in the genital area
- Refusal to go to school
- Delinquency/conduct problems
- Secretiveness
- Aspects of sexual molestation in drawings, games, fantasies
- Unusual aggressiveness or suicidal behavior

Parents can lessen or prevent their child's chances of being abused by ensuring their children are adequately educated about this issue.

Discussions should start as early as when they can understand concepts. Children must be taught to say "No" to an unwanted touch or any other behavior that makes them feel funny. Make your child aware of the difference between good and bad touch.

Parents should know who their children are spending time with. In most cases, the sexual predator is someone the child knows and trusts. Always have the communication lines open with your kids, so they feel free enough to report any such incidences. Take the time to reassure your child that she has done nothing wrong. Let your children know that you will do whatever you can to keep them safe. Also, let them you love them no matter what.

It is imperative to give your child enough time and attention so that she does not seek it elsewhere. Lonely and vulnerable children are the perfect targets for sexual predators. Children who are neglected and not emotionally secure will give in to anything to get that little attention.

If you suspect your child is being abused or know that she has been a victim in the past, offer her professional help in the form of a therapist or counselor.

Being understood and protected are the two most crucial factors in helping children deal with the trauma of sexual abuse. You need to do whatever it takes to ensure your child's current and future safety because your child counts on you to be there and keep her safe.

Helping Children Cope with Parent Illness

It is a very overwhelming situation for both parents and children when the parent is diagnosed with a serious illness. It is natural for families facing a new illness to be upset and worried about how they will deal with this crisis in their lives. These concerns may be more significant for families of young children or adolescents as they wonder how their children will cope with the uncertainty this diagnosis produces.

Sheila came to me concerned over whether she should tell her ten-year-old daughter Tracy about her recent breast cancer diagnosis. She was unsure how Tracy would handle it and the best way to bring up the matter with her.

How a child reacts to a parent's illness will depend a great deal upon how the parent and other adults who are close to the child deal with the crisis. Many times, parents attempt to shield their children from the pain of knowing about their diagnosis and hide the truth from their children. However, inevitably children sense something is seriously wrong even if they do not know precisely what it is. If a child hears of a parent's illness from an outsider, it will hurt the child more and break the child's trust in the parent.

Children can cope much better with the crisis if they can understand and be involved in what is happening.

A child's age is an essential factor to keep in mind when discussing the issue with him. The basic guideline is to tell the child the

77

truth to help him understand and be prepared for any changes that are going to take place in the family. Young children below the age of eight need not be given too detailed information. Children between the ages of eight and twelve understand serious illnesses and their consequences. Therefore, it is best to be straightforward but sensitive with them.

All children need to be given information about the name of the illness,

how it will be treated, and how their lives will be affected by it.

Sometimes children blame themselves for the parent's illness. This issue needs to be handled immediately by reassuring the child that the illness has nothing to do with him.

Teenagers are going through their confusions and stresses. Thus, the way they react to a parent's illness may be more intense than others. Also, since teenagers are trying to establish their independence, they may have difficulty expressing their feelings. They may react to this situation by being angry, irritable, moody, depressed, and pretend they are coping well, when in fact, they are filled with feelings of fear. It is best to give teens time to deal with the pain, expect mood changes, and encourage them to talk about their feelings. However, be open if they want to speak to someone else instead. Let them know that you understand how difficult this is for them.

It is also vital for parents to be open with their feelings about this issue. You can express to your children that you are also sad and hurt about the illness. Parents must pick a time to speak to the children when they are feeling calm themselves. If the parent is feeling distressed, it might be a good idea to wait until the emotions are a bit under control before speaking to the children. It is also helpful if both parents speak to the children together.

If parents feel that their child is finding it extremely difficult to cope with their illness and is displaying an extreme behavior change, it can help to talk to the child's school counselor or a mental health professional who can work with the child to help him cope.

There is nothing more painful for a family than if one family member is diagnosed with a serious illness. It is a challenge for parents to help children cope with this trauma while dealing with their uncertainties and fears. However, the love and support that family members provide each other can help them deal with this challenging time.

Helping Children Deal with Death

One of the most painful events youth can experience is the death of a friend. Parents often wish they could do more to take the pain away. As tough as these times are for the kids, the experience makes them wiser, kinder, and more compassionate. How you deal with children in a crisis will depend a lot on the specific circumstances, your child's age, needs, and ability to understand. However, certain basic guidelines apply.

- **Find your sense of optimism.** In troubled times, children pick up on what we are feeling more than anything else. We must strive to find a way to affirm life for them, even if we cannot yet do it for ourselves.

- **Listen to your child's feelings.** Children often have feelings in response to friends they have lost. It is outside your power to make everything better, but you can give your children the priceless gift of listening.

- **Give your child the necessary information in simple, positive terms.** It is vital to give your child information about what has happened. Use concrete language. Euphemisms confuse more than they cushion the pain. Tailor your explanations to your child's age and ability to understand. Children can be confused by elaborate explanations they cannot comprehend.

- **Reassure your children about what will happen to them.** Children interpret experiences in terms of themselves. They ask questions like, "Will that happen to me?" Respond to children's concerns by giving concrete answers and reassuring them that these mishaps do not happen with everyone and that you will take care of them.

- **Help your kids in the way they need.** It is much more helpful to ask questions than to give advice. Statements such as, "Help me understand how this is for you" bring us eye-opening responses. Instead of deciding what you can do to help kids feel better, *ask* them. Sometimes the efforts we employ to make children feel better may be less effective because they may not meet their needs.

- **Facilitate your kids to have closure.** Memorial services allow children an opportunity to say goodbye. Sometimes, administrators have school-based memorial events. This provides an opportunity for students to remember positive things about the friend who has passed. Speaking to the deceased friend's parents is extremely helpful. Ask your child to state her feelings to the parents, such as, "I liked the way she was always _____." "I'll miss doing _____ with her." It is also beneficial to invite some of your child's friends over and help them share their favorite memories of their friend who passed.

- **Use the situation as an opportunity for teaching.** In dealing with inevitable life crises, you can teach your children about the healthy expression of feelings, the positive aspects of change, and the human capacity to persevere and continue loving through hard times. Dealing constructively with the disequilibria caused by a loved one's death can provide important lessons for children that they can call on throughout their lives.

Parents must help their children through the grieving process.

You must help them grow and cope with the tragedy.

With your support, they will see that although their friend will always have a special place in their hearts, the sadness that once encompassed their daily lives will evolve into the joy of remembering the little things they shared. Discuss things with your kids that they remember and keep the pictures on the wall. You need to keep in mind that your children, no matter how young, feel the loss, and it is essential to talk about those feelings and ease their fears. As adults, we have a tough enough time dealing with death; with children, it is even harder!

Key Points

➢ Many children welcome a younger sibling. However, some of them can react adversely due to the insecurity they feel.

➢ Children living in homes full of aggression often display poor academic skills.

➢ Children caught in a cycle of family anger lack social skills and develop low self-esteem and depression.

➢ There is no doubt that children who are caught in the cycle of family anger are victims and may present their family experiences in their school and other settings.

➢ The purpose of sibling fights is to gain a parent's attention and support or show superiority and power over one another.

➢ Spend time teaching your children healthy ways to resolve conflicts.

➢ CONSISTENCY…CONSISTENCY…CONSISTENCY!

- ➢ Divorce can throw the child's entire life into a whirlwind. Divorce can adversely affect a child in terms of their behavior, school, relationships, and self-esteem.

- ➢ Children often feel like no one understands them and thus harm themselves to deal with the sense of emptiness they experience.

- ➢ Children fail to realize that cutting is only temporary relief from the emotional pain they are experiencing.

- ➢ Parents can lessen or prevent their child's chances of being abused by ensuring their children are adequately educated about this issue.

- ➢ Children can cope much better with the crisis if they can understand and be involved in what is happening.

- ➢ All children need to be given information about the name of the illness, how it will be treated, and how their lives will be affected by it.

➤ Parents must help their children through the grieving process. You must help them grow and cope with the tragedy.

Section 4: Navigating our World

Talking to Your Children About the News

Keeping up to date with the news can be incredibly beneficial for children and probably one of the most important habits parents try to teach them.

The average news broadcast contains as much violence, and action as many of the most popular entertainment shows on TV. However, unlike these shows, the news is real. Used properly, the news can teach children many positive things about the world. Simultaneously, the daily news can perpetuate stereotypes, confuse, anger, and even frighten children.

Parents bear the responsibility to decide what news is appropriate for their children. Research shows that children, especially those between the ages of eight and twelve, want their parents to talk with them about world issues. As children enter adolescence, they want to have a caring adult in their lives to talk about these matters.

Children under the age of six have a limited ability to discern the difference between the fantasy of an entertainment show and the reality of the news. Kids in this age range are likely to fear what they see on the news. Use caution when you allow a preschooler to be exposed to the news without supervision.

Psychologically, kids between the ages of six and ten are the most vulnerable to what they see on the news. At this age, the kids know the difference between fantasy and reality but lack perspective. During this time, it is essential to watch the news with your child.

Adolescents (ages eleven and up) have a better understanding of fact and fiction and expand their perspectives. Their constant exposure to media and the news can lead to confusion and having conflicting information. You cannot monitor everything your teens are exposed to, but it is imperative to check in with them about news and other media.

Following are some tips to help you talk to your kids about the news:

- **Create an Open Dialogue**. The best way to check in with your children about the exposures they are getting is by talking to them about what they see and hear. You must speak with your kids openly and honestly. Use encouragement, support, and positive reinforcement so your kids know they can ask any question on any topic freely and without fear of consequence. Provide straightforward answers. Otherwise, your child may make up her explanations that can be more frightening than any honest response you could offer. If your child appears depressed or angry by what he saw on the news, make sure you speak to him right away.

- **Acknowledge Your Child's Fears**. The fears that some news stories bring out in your children are genuine. That is why it is essential to reassure your children that people are working to ensure their worlds remain safe. Let your kids know that just because they saw something on the news does not mean it will happen to them.
- **Explore the Facts with Your Child**. At times, it may be necessary to provide your child with more factual information than what is provided in the news report. This will give them a greater perspective concerning the issues and help reduce their fears.
- **Select Child-Friendly News Sources for Your Child**. There are some children's television channels that report on issues kids care about in a way they can understand. There are also many websites and magazines dedicated to news for kids.

Raising a child is one of the most gratifying experiences you will ever have and one of the toughest. Try as you might to be the best parent you can; our complex world challenges you every day with disturbing issues that are difficult for children to understand and for parents to explain. However, communication with your child and the perspective you provide help promote healthy growth for your children's minds.

Television Violence and Children

Research has found most children plug into the world of television long before they enter school.

Children spend more time learning about life through media more than from any other source. The average child spends approximately twenty-eight hours a week watching television, which is twice as much time as he spends in school.

I went to watch a movie with a friend. It was a great movie but had quite a lot of violent content in it. Upon looking around, I noticed many families had brought along their little kids, which got me thinking about whether these parents were aware of the harm television violence has on their children's minds and behaviors?

Children are known to imitate behaviors they are exposed to.

My nine-year-old son will often surprise me by narrating a piece of dialogue from an advertisement or a line from his favorite cartoon show. Thus, there is a great risk of children imitating the violent behavior projected in movies or television programs that they view.

Due to the heat and constant rain in Miami, children tend to spend more time in front of the television, which is increasingly dominated by violent content. I was aghast watching a cartoon channel with my nephews who were visiting me a few months back. Derogatory and demeaning words were being casually and recurrently used by the characters, thus reducing the seriousness of using this offensive language.

Hundreds of studies done on the effects of television violence on children have found that children may:

1. Become "immune" to the horror of violence.
2. Start using violence to solve their problems.
3. Imitate the violent acts observed by them, and the language heard.
4. Begin identifying with certain violent characters or victims, thus affecting their emotional well-being.

The effects of television violence on children may not always be evident immediately. It can show up several years later. Longitudinal research studies following viewing habits and behavior patterns of children have found that young boys who viewed the most violent programs growing up were the most likely to engage in aggressive and delinquent behavior and serious criminal behavior later in life.

So, what can we do to help reduce the impact of television violence on our children?

- Parents need to pay attention to the kinds of programs their children are viewing. Try not to have a TV in your child's bedroom to aid in this process. Also, you can preview the programs before allowing your children to be exposed to the same.

- Set appropriate limits on television viewing time and the programs that are acceptable.

- Co-viewing and commenting on the television content diminishes its impact since it reduces children's chances of identifying with those characters and imitating behaviors displayed. If something you disapprove of is shown, you can shut off the television immediately and use this opportunity to discuss with your children whether the violent acts were the appropriate way of dealing with the situation and what better ways are there of dealing with challenging situations.

- Show your disapproval of violent behaviors and teach your children healthy ways of resolving conflicts.

- Set a good example by limiting your own television viewing time.

- Offer your children fun alternatives to television like playing board games, reading, working on craft activities, practicing playing a musical instrument, or learn some new dance steps. This will also ensure quality time is spent with your children.

- Ensure that you understand the movies' rating before you head for a night out at the movies with your little ones.

Everything that children see or hear in the media affects them in some way.

Unfortunately, violent content has become one of the popular forms of entertainment in recent times. It is creating a whole generation that seems to believe that beating the s*** out of someone is the only way of resolving conflicts.

Let us pause for a moment and think about whether it is worth taking our children to the movies and exposing them to malicious content just because we want to entertain three hours of our lives? Also, let us ponder over the value that we are adding to our children's lives, allowing them to be stuck in front of the TV so we can get them out of our hair or keep them unrewardingly engaged? If your answer to both the above is negative, let us all do our best to keep our children away from the ills of media violence.

Getting "Webbed" on the Web

Whatever your age, the Internet is an excellent place for fun. It is not only entertaining, but it lets you keep in touch with friends and family and provides an enormous amount of information.

However, this fascinating technology is not hazard-free. Every day, youngsters are being exploited on the Internet by receiving information that they are too young for or being drawn into unhealthy relationships. Teenagers are most likely to get into trouble online because they like to explore cyberspace. They are more likely to reach out to people outside of their immediate peer groups, and, sadly, they are more often preyed upon as victims by pedophiles and other exploiters.

Talk to your child about what he can and cannot do online. By setting reasonable guidelines, parents can help their kids take advantage of all the positive aspects of the Internet while avoiding most of its pitfalls. Discuss these rules and post them near the computer as a reminder. Remember to monitor their compliance with these rules, especially regarding the amount of time your children spend on the computer. A child or teenager's excessive use of online services, especially late at night, maybe a clue that there is a potential problem.

It is not uncommon for people to make "friends" in chat rooms. You enter a room, start a conversation with someone, and before you know it, you have established a relationship of sorts. People sometimes use chat rooms to exploit others. Monitor the amount of time your children spend chatting and who their online friends are.

Never allow a child to arrange a face-to-face meeting with someone she met online without parental permission. If a meeting is arranged, make the first one in a public spot, and be sure to accompany your child.

Make Internet browsing a family activity. Consider keeping the computer in a family room rather than the child's bedroom. Learn everything you can about the Internet. When children are exposed to technology at a young age, parents often find themselves lagging their children in computer skills. Surprisingly, this may be the key to your involvement. What better way to learn about the Internet than to do so alongside your child?

There are services that rate websites for content and filtering programs and browsers that empower parents to block the types of sites they consider inappropriate.

Ask your teenager to never respond to messages or bulletin board items that are suggestive, obscene, threatening, or that make them feel uncomfortable. There are a lot of websites that entice the immature and the vulnerable. Encourage your children to tell you if they encounter such messages. If they tell you about someone or something unpleasant they experienced, your first response should not be to blame them or take away their Internet privileges. Work with them to help them avoid problems in the future. Remember, how you respond will determine whether they confide in you the next time they encounter an issue and how they learn to deal with issues independently.

Tell your children not to give out personal information such as an address, telephone number, parent's work address/telephone number or schedule, or their school's name and location without your permission. Also, establish that they cannot post their pictures online without your consent. Emphasize the importance of never exchanging photographs with people they do not know. They need to clearly understand that people on the Internet may not be who they appear to be.

The power of computers and the Internet has provided families with unprecedented communication tools, learning, and having fun. With this power comes the responsibility of supervising the use of these tools to preserve family values.

Educate yourself and your children on the dangers of using the Internet to ensure that you take advantage of the net as a resource while protecting your children.

The Social Dilemma

For a while, I lead a support group for moms of teenage girls. One topic that was discussed more than any other in the group was "Social Media." It is hard to imagine a life without Facebook, Instagram, Snapchat, and Twitter. While there are some benefits to connecting with your friends or with like-minded peers who have shared interests with a click of a button, the world of social media is not free from dangers.

For young minds, these dangers are exasperated as they find themselves constantly comparing their lives to those of their peers and finding it falling short. The moms in the group relayed of their girls were being bullied on social media while others were sexting with strangers they met online. Others were, in their opinion, addicted to these platforms.

The adverse psychological effects of social media can include severe isolation, anxiety, depression, and sometimes suicide. It is essential that we as parents are informed and vigilant about our children's social media use. The following are some tips for parents to help ensure that our children are enjoying social media safely:

• Educate yourself on all the social media platforms that your children might potentially want to be on. Read reviews, age requirements and, any other details that might help you familiarize yourself with the platform.

• Be mindful of your own social media usage and the effects it might have on you. If you feel insecure when you see your friend having "the perfect vacation," your children will pick up on that and may feel and display similar insecurities.

• Keep a close eye on who your child is befriending on social media platforms. We know that there are people on there who could hurt our children, so monitoring your child's interactions is very necessary.

• Understand that cyberbullying is a real thing and kids can be as mean to someone online as in person. Watch out for signs that your child is being bullied.

• Inform yourself about 'Facebook Depression.' This is when our children compare themselves and their lives to the happy, glamorous faces and lives of their peers and experience a low sense of self. Talk to them about the reality that no one posts about when they are sad or experience failure, but that does not mean they do not.

• Children, nowadays as young as 9 or 10, are using social media platforms even though most platform's age requirements are older. Just because other parents are ok with their children using social media, you do not have to feel pressured into allowing your child to do the same.

• Set limits on social media usage for the week. Also, you can set rules about where they are around you when on social media platforms.

• Keep the channels of communication with your child open. Talk to your children about the dangers of social media and safety. Let your children know that they can always come to you with any questions or help if they need it.

The world of social media is ever-changing and navigating through it all can be overwhelming for parents. We cannot always be there with our children to keep them safe; however, building the trust in your children that they can come to you any time they find themselves in an unsafe situation is the key to truly protecting them.

Teaching Children to be Money Wise

Back in our childhood days, we can all probably recall a time when our parents denied us a particular toy or a favorite treat while shopping. It was a very heartbreaking experience. After all, we thought our moms and dads had an unlimited supply of that green paper which they would give the nice lady at the check-out counter so that we could have whatever our heart desired. That was our perception of home finances at that age. Mom or Dad simply pulled out a magic piece of paper, and we had a new toy or a pair of shoes.

As adults, we now know all too well that there is no magic behind a bank account and credit card. However, too small children may still appear to be a combination of Santa Claus and a magic Genie who makes money appear out of thin air.

How do you explain the truth about home finances to children?

How do we make our kids responsible for handling money?

Like most life lessons we try to teach our kids, financial responsibility is based primarily on habits that lead to positive or negative results. The sooner you start building healthy financial habits within your kids, the earlier they establish realistic thinking about money. For example, if Ray spends all his allowance four days before his next one is due, his "need" for the latest play station game will just have to wait. If, however, he has learned to save a portion of his previous allowance, the game can be his, thanks to his long-term planning.

It is never too early to start teaching children

about responsibilities and money management.

Starting as early as age five, a child can be responsible for simple daily chores around the house. This will teach your child the critical reality of life that one must work to make money. The chores can be such tasks as folding the clothes or making the bed. Whatever the chores are, make sure they are reasonable for your child to accomplish. The next step is to decide upon a daily allowance your child will receive upon completing the chores.

Teach your child to manage his money by dividing it into three sections: for the future, for the present, and for giving. Have a small box for each of the above and decorate them according to what they will represent. The future box will represent savings for the future. Cover it with pictures representing his future goals like buying a guitar or music system. The present-box is for anything that your child may want to buy immediately, which is not in your budget for him.

Finally, explain to your child the importance of giving. Talk about what organizations your child can help with that money or what gifts he can buy for someone in need. This box could be decorated to reflect the many ways of giving to others. At the end of each week, your child will divide the money up into the three boxes. Once money has accumulated, take your child to the bank and have him watch you deposit money into a savings account.

Remember that the skills you teach your child today will pay off for years to come.

Your child is not just learning to budget allowance; he is learning to plan and understand how decisions impact each other. These are incredibly valuable skills that can be learned as early as three or four years of age and sharpened with years of use. Once the preliminary work is done in setting up a system of handling money, your child will follow through.

Parental guidance will help your child become a responsible adult

and will help him gain money management skills which will last a lifetime!

Key Points

➤ Keeping up to date with the news can be incredibly beneficial for children and probably one of the most important habits parents try to teach their wards.

➤ Create an Open Dialogue

➤ Acknowledge Your Child's Fears

➤ Explore the Facts with Your Child

➤ Select Child-Friendly News Sources for Your Child

➤ Research has found most children plug into the world of television long before they enter school.

➤ Children are known to imitate behavior that they are exposed to.

➤ Everything that children see or hear in the media affects them in some way.

➤ Educate yourself and your children on the dangers of using the Internet and social media to ensure that you take advantage of the Internet as a resource while protecting your children.

➢ Remember that the skills you teach your child today will pay off for years to come.

➢ It is never too early to start teaching children about responsibilities and money management.

➢ Parental guidance will help your child become a responsible adult and help him gain money management skills that will last a lifetime!

Section 5: Encouraging Positive Behavior

Creative Answers to Misbehavior Part 1

Discipline has been described in many ways, with an equal number of different ideas for when and how a child should be held accountable for his behavior. Discipline is more effectively used to provide consequences for your child's behavior that will encourage him to behave more appropriately in the future. Since I started my practice, I have had at least two to three parents come in every week regarding discipline issues with their children.

When picking a disciplining strategy, ask yourself, "Is this disciplinary strategy the most effective strategy for achieving what you need to accomplish?" If you want to teach your child how to read, you cannot discipline him for not reading, nor would you discipline a child for crying at bedtime when she does not have the skills of soothing herself to sleep on her own. It is essential to have a clear understanding of what behaviors you want to see your child display, how those behaviors are taught, and how to tell if your child's misbehavior is due to a lack of skill or intentional action.

One of the questions I am asked more frequently about discipline is, "At what age should we start to discipline?" The answer is quite simple: When your child starts engaging in behaviors that you disapprove of and that they can be reasonably expected to refrain from. You will need to be mindful to differentiate between behavior that is developmentally appropriate for your child, and that is intentional and inappropriate. For example, an infant spitting out his first bite of rice cereal is developmentally appropriate.

A second and equally important question is, "Is there an alternative way of encouraging the child to engage in behaviors that you feel are important?" If, for example, you are having difficulty getting your son to eat a balanced meal, instead of coming up with innovative methods to punish him for not eating his vegetables, you should figure out creative ways to encourage him to eat vegetables.

This two-part series will highlight some effective disciplinary measures that parents can use to curb misbehavior:

- One way to arrange a consequence is to simply keep a steady course and continue the ordinary routines that the child's misbehavior conflicts with. In other words, maintain routines and let the child, rather than yourself, experience the brunt of the inconvenience. For example, "I am sorry you are not ready to go with us to the mall, but you had plenty of advance notice. We are going to have to leave without you tonight; maybe next week will go better for you."

- Emphasize what you will do for the child or allow, in contrast to making the child do or not do something. Refuse to cooperate with the child in the typical arrangement of caring services until the child decides to stop misbehaving. For example, "I won't wash your clothes when they are lying on the floor in your room."

- One of the most common forms of misbehavior involves an attempted display of excessive personal power in the form of an invitation to a power struggle. When you confront the child and ask him to stop specific misbehavior, the child digs in, becomes more blatant, and defies you. By this process, the child lures you into a tug of war with words like, "Yes, you will/No I won't." The best procedure, in this case, is to refuse to engage in a power struggle. Sidestep power struggles by indicating your intent to reach a peaceful solution. You can tell your child something like, "I won't argue and debate with you about this. I want you to understand my real feelings, and I want to understand yours. When you are ready to do this, we can talk."

- Logical consequences for inappropriate behavior can be effective in disciplining children of all ages, especially older children. Logical consequences are those that follow because of the child's poor choice of behavior. You can often determine the logical outcome for a given situation if you asked yourself what would happen if you stepped back and did not intervene. It is crucial when using this discipline option to ensure that all caregivers are on the same page regarding which consequences are in place on any given day.

- You can also use the removal of privileges as a form of discipline for your child. A privilege is anything your child favors or desires more than the basic needs that you provide. Privileges can be playing with toys, video games, or friends, receiving a special treat, watching TV, or attending a social event.

106

The following five guidelines will help increase the effectiveness of this strategy.

1. Be careful about what you remove. Make sure that whatever privilege you choose to remove can be removed. If you remove the privilege of going to a movie, you must get a babysitter for that child if the rest of the family is going. Thus, choose a privilege that you can stick to.

2. If your rule is that the privilege is lost if your son swears, then the first swear word should result in a loss of privilege. Warning him that he will lose the privilege instead of removing it will increase misbehavior because he knows that you will not follow through with your threat.

3. Limit the length of time that the privilege is withheld. If your daughter uses a swear word at dinner, she loses her computer time after dinner. This should not affect whether she gets the computer the next night. The longer you take something away, the more likely you will forget, give it back, or allow your child to bargain with you to get it back.

4. Be prepared to vary the privileges you remove. If your child does not seem to upset about the privilege you remove, try removing a different privilege the next time he misbehaves.

5. If your child is socially isolated or has poor social skills, you may not want to remove privileges involving social activities as a

discipline strategy. Thus, choose watching TV or video game time as privileges to remove.

Misbehaviors need to be checked exceedingly early in a child's life.

If not, it tends to become a habit and a way of life.

Creative Answers to Misbehavior Part 2

In Part 1 of this series, we discussed some effective disciplining techniques to curb misbehavior among children.

Here are some more:

- One way children oppose disciplinary consequences is by starting a whole new set of issues. Their response to your limits becomes a separate disciplinary matter and forms a second layer of contention. Give the child a choice of how to respond to the consequences and avoid over-controlling. For example, you could tell your child, "You must go to your room now. Are you going to walk by yourself or do I carry you?" or "You can dawdle as much as you want to; you are simply not coming out of this room until it is cleaned up. It doesn't matter to me how long you stay in."

- Your child is more likely to go along with a disciplinary consequence when it seems "fair." Give your child "a voice and a choice" in arranging the consequence. You could ask your child, "You owe us money for breaking the flower vase. Either pay it now with the money you have saved, earn it by doing some extra work around the house, or we will hold back your next two allowances to pay for the damage. Which plan would you like to use?"

- Encourage children to make a sincere and meaningful apology, either written or verbal, to the offended person, if any after a misdeed. For example, "You owe your sister an apology for doing that. You can write to her if you wish. I will check with her at 8:00 and ask her if she has been apologized to by that time."

- When encouraging an apology, emphasize future improvements in the child's relationship with the offended person. For example, "You can't undo what you have done, but at least you can improve things for the future with your sister by being more careful with her things."

- Repayment means having the child repay for the physical, emotional, or other damage caused by a misdeed. In addition to teaching your child the importance of paying back through money for a broken flower vase, also teach him the importance of paying back others for any pain or inconvenience the misbehavior might have caused due to the sentiments involved with the flower vase. Perhaps, it was a gift from someone near and dear. You can tell your child, "The best way to mend someone's feelings and to compensate for the pain you caused her is by giving that person some joy. Do favors or good deeds for the person to show how sincere you are in wanting to make up for what you did. Apologizing was the first step and repaying for the flower vase you broke was the second. How about doing something nice for her now to make up for any pain you caused?"

· Suggest a better alternative to the misbehavior the next time. Simply telling the child to stop the misconduct or giving a consequence to stop it falls far short of addressing the underlying need the misbehavior was intended to meet.

It is important to give your child a substitute for the misbehavior –

a new and better way of behaving that will meet those exact needs.

For example, you could tell your child, "The next time Sarah bothers you like this, what would be a better thing to do than to hit her?" or "From now on, if you want to borrow your sister's CD player, what would be a better way of getting it rather than just sneaking into her room and taking it without her permission?"

- Explain to your child the merits of good behavior. Make sure the explanation is simple and easy to understand. You can use examples to explain why the desired improvements in the child's behavior for future similar situations are better than the misbehavior that the child has displayed; "If you get permission to use the CD player, you and your sister will both be happier and calmer, and there won't be much fighting between the two of you. Maybe she would also teach you all the features of the player and make it more fun for you to use it!"

Good discipline does not mean an endless parade of yelling, nagging, and punishment. It involves a heavy emphasis on preventing misbehavior and confronting it early, while you and the child are relatively calm.

Consequences of misbehavior are most effective when they are brief, prompt, reasonable, and logically tied to the misbehavior.

When you do this, your children are more likely to respond positively to your discipline and leadership and allow you to strengthen your bond of love and mutual respect gradually.

Helping Kids Behave Responsibly

"At three, little Jake is the apple of mom and dad's eye. Everything is done for him at home; he is not expected to lift a finger. After playing with his toys, he eats and goes to bed, leaving the clearing up for mom to take care of. She has not an ounce of complaint picking up after her precious little one.

At five, Jake is still not expected to help around the house when he messes it up during playtime since he still is only a baby!

111

At seven, mommy is beginning to get a little tired of constantly picking up after Jake but still thinks maybe her darling is too little to be helping her out.

At ten, mom has had it! Her days are spent yelling and screaming at Jake to pick up his toys, be conscientious about his things, and help around the house! She cannot comprehend why a ten-year-old cannot behave responsibly. She often complains to dad about Jake's irresponsible behavior, who is also confused about the reasons for his son's immaturity. Precious Jake does not seem to be paying heed at all."

Over the years, I have encountered countless such scenarios where parents are pulling out their hair over their children's lack of responsibility.

I have just one question for them,

"How can little Jake be responsible when this skill hasn't been taught to him?"

The first step to raising responsible children is to start young. Inculcating responsible behavior in children must begin when they are toddlers. They must be expected to pick up their toys after playtime. Children have a natural desire to help and to participate. As a toddler, children often ask to help. Encourage this behavior in your child and start the process of training for a lifetime of helpfulness.

Your role in developing responsibility in your child is critical. When teaching your child about a chore, offer help at the beginning to enable your child to understand and follow through. Chores must be assigned to all at home.

Children must be assigned chores depending upon their ability to perform the same. They must start simple and become more complex as the child grows older.

Some helpful techniques for parents to use when getting children involved in household chores are listed below:

- Explain to your child the list of chores they need to do and what constitutes a job well done. Describe how often the chores are to be done and the steps to be taken for successful completion. Children are much likely to follow through with a plan when they know precisely how to achieve results.
- Show faith in your child's capability in handling chores. This encouragement will go a long way in motivating your child.
- You can use a chores chart to help your child develop responsibility and eliminate the need for nagging. The chart can include the tasks for each family member, a method of marking when the task is completed, and points or rewards for completion.
- To add variety, chores can be rotated weekly so that no family member feels that they have been treated unfairly.
- One of the most common methods to get your child to perform chores is to set a special time when all the family members work

together. The goal is to let the child see that everyone is involved, which will help him associate work with pleasure and family unity.

- Offer little surprise incentives for the completion of a chore successfully. These can include special privileges like an extra helping of dessert or an extra hour of playtime and given at random to the child.

- Be sensitive to your child's needs. If your child does not want to complete his chores on any one day, show empathy and understand what your child is complaining about. Discuss your child's concern and address it lovingly and helpfully.

- Be consistent in expecting the child to complete his chores. Often parents excuse children from completing their chores when they have homework to do or a test. However, it is essential to note that there is no reason why a child cannot manage his time to complete the assigned homework and still contribute to completing the chores.

We all want children to behave responsibly. Homes where routines and systems are clear and where each family member participates in keeping the home clean and healthy are happy homes. By having a positive attitude, you can help your child prepare for adult responsibilities successfully and teach them that work does not have to be a burden. You must develop a system that works, keeping in mind the needs of your family. The result will be an orderly home and mature, responsible family members!

Discouraging Aggression in Children

Sam was constantly getting into fights on the playground with the other boys. One day, he slammed a boy's hand at the door that left him with a fracture. The school authorities and the parents were in total dismay about how to handle the problem.

Aggression in a child is one of the most problematic issues a parent can face. At school, aggressive behaviors prompt more phone calls to parents than any other problem. Aggression in a young child may indicate an increased risk of future issues as well. Young children who regularly engage in physical fights are three times more likely to be diagnosed later with a mental health problem than children who do not.

So, how does aggressive behavior develop?

One primary source of such behavior is the way parents model behavior and treat their children. Parents who threaten, yell, berate, and beat their children as a measure of disciplining them often have children who deal with their frustration in the same way. Other factors that correlate highly to children's aggressive behavior include TV violence, violent video games, movies, child maltreatment, unresponsive schooling, and economic inequality.

Parents can help monitor and eliminate factors that influence aggressive behavior. The following are some suggestions for modifying your behavior and your child's environment to reduce aggressive behavior in your child:

- **Model Good Anger Management Skills:** Parents who model good anger management skills and help children learn skills for dealing with angry feelings are much more likely to control their emotions.

- **Eliminate Physical Punishment, Yelling, and Swearing as a Means of Disciplining Your Child:** Children who are most likely to be aggressive are the ones being subjected to the strongest punishment. The act of spanking results in increased aggression among children. Spanking does not teach the child anything. Instead, the child might end up feeling like they must hit every time they are angry. Yelling and swearing seem to have the same effect on children as spanking. Thus, parents must monitor their yelling and swearing and eliminate these behaviors in front of their children even if these are not directed at them.

- **Avoid Direct Confrontation:** Some parent-child relationships seem to consist of one altercation after the other. Each interaction escalates to a battle of wills in a matter of minutes, often resulting in yelling, arguing, threats, or physical aggression. Aggressive children seem to thrive on confrontations. If you use confrontation to get your child to do or not to do something, your child will learn very quickly he needs to do the same to have his needs met. This is typically not effective and teaches your child behaviors that you most likely do not want him to display with you or with others.

- **Give Appropriate Consequences for Aggressive Behavior:** Ignoring children's negative behaviors or responding inappropriately may teach them that aggression works. Some parents arrange their lives and their children's lives to avoid as many chances for aggression as possible. Children who can get their way by acting aggressively with no repercussions are encouraged to continue being aggressive. Withholding privileges or being grounded for a specific time are strategies parents can use as consequences for aggressive behavior.

- **Restrict Violent Media, Games, and Playmates:** It is essential to monitor how much time the child spends watching TV or their iPad and what he watches. You should also supervise the number of hours your child spends playing video games or computer games, especially those with violent content. Your child's friends can also influence aggressive behavior. Children should not be allowed to physically "work it out" when they disagree. Teach your child effective conflict management.

- **Teach Your Child Ways to Cope with Frustration and Anger:** One helpful anger management skill is the use of a "competing response," which is a behavior that is difficult to do when you are angry. Teach your child controlled breathing, counting to 100, or other grounding techniques to distract him and reduce his anger.

Aggression in children is often a symptom of the environment in which the child is being raised. When parents play rough with their children, argue with them or in front of them, approach them aggressively, and use spanking as their primary method of discipline, they often have aggressive children. The key to dealing with an aggressive child is to remove the elements that contribute to the aggressive behavior and to teach the child alternate ways of coping with anger.

Why Children Lie

Children lying is perhaps one of the most serious concerns parents have. We all want our children to be truthful. Lying may cause difficulties for children at school and with their friends, disrupt family life, and lay the groundwork for adulthood problems. A distraught father expressed his concerns about his twelve-year-old daughter, "Samantha is a compulsive liar. She can lie, looking you straight in the eye. If you did not know her well enough, you would easily believe she was telling the truth. I am at my wits' end with her. All I need her to do is stop lying."

The question is, where do children like Samantha learn to lie?

Although dishonesty can be seen on television and witnessed on the school playground, children's first lessons about lying behavior are usually taught at home. Those little white lies about not being home when an acquaintance calls who you do not wish to speak to, or the one about the gift your relative gave you that you simply detest despite the smile on your face—well, they all add up in your child's eyes. Thus, parental

118

behavior can sometimes teach children that lying is better than telling the truth.

Whenever possible, keep your word. Always explain and apologize if you must break a promise. If you find yourself lying in front of your child, be sure to talk about it with her and clarify your reasons and values explaining the lie. If you made a mistake by telling a lie, admit it.

Children usually lie either to avoid punishment or to get attention and recognition. If a child breaks a lamp, admits the truth, and receives a punishment, the child will feel that it would have been better to lie about the incident. When a parent is too rigid or strict, and the children believe that what they have done would anger their parents, they would try their best to cover up the facts not to upset them. Then the first time they get away with it, it simply encourages them to try it again and again until it becomes a habit.

The wise parent, in this case, would say, "I'm sure you didn't mean to break the lamp. I am proud of you for owning up to your mistake. I know you are going to be more careful in the future. However, since I am going to have to buy a new lamp, I want you to help me pay for it with your pocket money." Children who are recognized for telling the truth grow up to be more truthful. Excessive or irrational punishments may backfire. The greater the fear of punishment, the less likely your child is going to "fess up" the next time.

Punishing a child for lying can be risky since it could be the primary motivator for the child lying in the first place. If you are to discipline your child for dishonesty, make sure the punishment is the natural and logical consequence of the dishonest behavior. For example, it may be appropriate that a child who has repeatedly lied about getting her homework done must bring a note home from her teacher daily until trust is restored. This consequence makes sense to the child considering the behavior you are trying to change.

Some lies are told to get attention. Children often learn that the more fascinating the lie is, the more attention they will get. In this case, question the child once and only once. If your child lies to get your attention, do not accuse the child of being a liar, but do not pretend like you are not aware of it, either. Make it clear that you do not believe she completed all her homework in fifteen minutes but that you love her anyway. If your child tells a lie to someone else and you witness it, do not point it out in front of the other person. Wait until you are alone with your child and then discuss it.

Lying concerns all parents. Once the cycle of lying and distrust is in full swing, it is difficult to find a single way in which the cycle may be stopped. Thus, it is fundamental for every parent to think through why a child lies and then determine how to stop the behavior as soon as possible.

We all need to teach our children to learn to love the truth and not be fearful of and thus hide it!

Stealing in Children

Tina is continuously stealing. She steals from her friends, family members, and home. Whenever asked about stealing, she denies having done it. Everyone knows that she is lying.

Stealing is typical but inappropriate behavior in school-aged children. While some severe forms of stealing can indicate a more serious psychological problem, most of the time, it is simply a behavior that will be outgrown. Sometimes, children steal to have things the family cannot otherwise afford. Other times, they steal to get attention and win friends through material possessions, and still other times, it is due to peer pressure and the need to "fit in."

Parents need to view the whole situation and decide the probable cause for the behavior. If the child is stealing to attract attention because they feel neglected, you must rectify that situation by providing your child with the needed emotional security. On the other hand, if the child is stealing to win friends or peer pressure, they need to be spoken to about forming meaningful friendships. Parents must bear in mind that in addition to taking care of the cause, they must also deal with the actual behavior of stealing.

So, what can parents do to deal with the behavior of stealing before it becomes a serious issue?

Remember that attempting to get a child to accept that they have taken something that belongs to someone else is usually futile. Children know that stealing is wrong. It is hard for a child who has stolen something to admit to having done it. Ask the child once, and if the child denies having stolen, do not press the issue.

Parents must decide in their minds whether their child is likely to have taken the item. If there is a reasonable possibility of the child having stolen, decide on the appropriate course of action. If there is any major uncertainty about whether the child has stolen, you should give them the benefit of the doubt and drop the issue.

If you decide that the child has stolen, some appropriate actions include telling the child, "Although you have denied taking the item, I have good reason to suspect that you did take it. Because of this, you are grounded for two nights." You could also take away a privilege such as their phone, hanging out with friends, or attending some major event they have been excited about. If the child starts arguing about being innocent, simply tell your child that if it turns out that you are wrong, you will apologize. Do not discuss the matter with your child again but move to implement the consequence.

If your child admits to having taken something that belongs to someone else, he should be instructed to return the item to its rightful owner. This should apply even if the child has stolen something from a grocery or department store. Forcing the child to face the store owner is perhaps the best corrective measure a parent can use in a situation like this. There is usually no need for additional punishment in this case.

If the child steals the second time, repeat the procedure. This time, however, additional restrictions may be in order. In the vast majority of cases, this procedure will solve the problem. However, if the stealing does not stop and is accompanied by other behavioral issues, make an appointment with a counselor or therapist to understand the root cause of the behavior and discuss strategies to stop it.

Parents have a huge responsibility to ensure that their children grow up to be valued individuals of society. Learning about the right and wrong actions early in life will help your children be model citizens!

Children Who Swear

It is shocking for parents to hear their innocent and sweet children suddenly start using swear words as part of their conversation. This is a highly prevalent problem that often perplexes parents about the "how and why" their child's vocabulary has suddenly expanded to include these terrible words.

Usually, children begin swearing when they have heard adults doing the same. We all know kids are like sponges who absorb everything they see and hear in their environment. They may be copying mom, dad, another adult, a sibling, or friends at school. Sometimes, children also swear to get attention. Younger kids are looking for their parent's attention, and swearing is one surefire way of getting it. Teenagers sometimes swear to "fit in" or be part of the group. If their friends are all doing it, they feel like they must do it, too. They often believe that it is cool to swear.

The first thing to do when you observe your child swearing is to check your language. It is not fair to expect your children not to use these words if you are extensively using them.

Kids always model parent behaviors; thus, if you want them to monitor their language,

you must monitor yours.

If you are not using foul language, try to investigate the other sources that might influence your child's vocabulary, like television, friends, neighbors, or relatives. Try to keep your child away from the source as much as possible. If your child is picking up foul language at school or on the bus, speak to the school authorities about what they can do to help.

Establish clear rules about swearing with your child. Make it clear to your child that such words are not permissible at home. If your child uses these words when angry, try to teach him healthy ways of expressing emotions, especially when he is frustrated or angry. This is especially true for younger children who most likely do not understand the meaning of the words they use. Also, explaining to children the meaning of the words usually makes them stop since they now understand the vulgarity of the expressions.

Do not feed your child's bad habit. If your kids are swearing to get attention, yelling at them, or reprimanding them in any other way will increase the frequency of the behavior. A calmer approach usually works here. Ignore your child's behavior at that time and instead give him attention when behaving in a desired manner.

Praise is also an immensely powerful tool for parents to use to help their kids get over the habit of swearing. Study after study has shown that if a child is praised for a specific behavior, it is more likely to happen again. Thus, praising good and appropriate language will increase the frequency of its occurrence.

An excellent technique to help children stop swearing is to use the "swear box." Explain to your kids that every time they swear, they must drop some money out of their savings into the box. This very often helps children keep a check on the use of swear words.

Children typically outgrow this pattern in time. However, sometimes children need a bit of help to get over this habit. Talk to your child's school counselor or a therapist if your efforts are not paying off. It is always ok to seek help from others. It is very distressing for parents to hear their kids use inappropriate language.

Educate your children about the power of language

and its effect on the people around them.

125

It is not easy being a good parent; we all know this, but we need to try our best to understand our children and guide them in their formative years to have a comfortable future.

Managing Your Child's Behavior Away from Home

All behavior programs tend to break down when away from home. Many parents are frustrated because their little ones will not cooperate in a supermarket or amusement center. The most critical step in dealing with this very distressing situation is to be sure not to relax your discipline efforts simply because you are distracted by other activities at hand.

It is not uncommon when you are at the grocery store's check-out counter for your toddler to reach out for a candy bar. At this point, you must take the candy bar away and, in a neutral voice, say something like, "No, Jack. You are not allowed to take candy from there." DO NOT give in to the resulting tantrum, no matter how embarrassed you are, and you will teach your toddler a valuable lesson. If you give the candy back to him or keep it, you teach your child to do the same thing the next time he has the opportunity.

Do not worry about what other people are thinking; just concentrate on getting your child's behavior under control. I know this is easier said than done; however, at that moment, this is the best alternative.

If you are faced with having to discipline your child while in a store or any other public place, you can just carry your toddler out of the store and into the car until he calms down and then go back for the stuff. You must **not** give in to his tantrums. Once the consequence is served and he is calm, you may acknowledge his feelings by saying something like, "I know you love candy, but that does not mean you take it without getting permission to do so. The rule is you ask for what you want, and mommy decides whether you get it this time or the next."

If your child is older, take a moment to explain the rules before entering a public place. Tell your child, for example, that you are going to the store to purchase some food for dinner tonight and that you will not be buying anything for him. You can also tell him that you understand how much he may want something during the shopping trip, but he must wait for another time. Tell him to please stay close to you and keep his hands off items in the store. When you are shopping, frequently talk with him and thank him for doing as you have asked. You could also offer them a reward based on his conduct in the store. For example, you could tell him that if he stays close to you and does not touch anything, you will allow him to watch cartoons for a half-hour extra.

Another way to avoid tantrum scenes is by keeping your child involved in helping you shop throughout the trip and unload the cart at the end. Hand the items to him one at a time so that he can drop them into the cart. This will keep your child occupied.

Public outings with your child can be pleasant experiences if you keep in mind that your child is learning the whole time he is there, and you are the one responsible for what he learns. In addition to teaching your child about the types of fruits at the grocery store you must teach him how to be polite and follow directions when there.

If you successfully impart to your child the basic behaviors expected of him when at public places, you can surely make every trip an enjoyable and learning experience!

Key Points

➤ Misbehaviors need to be checked early on in a child's life. If not, it tends to become a habit and a way of life.

➤ It is essential to give your child a substitute for misbehavior – a new and better way of behaving that will meet those exact needs.

➤ Consequences of misbehavior are most effective when they are brief, prompt, reasonable, and logically tied to the misconduct.

➤ I have just one question for them, "How can little Jake be responsible when this skill hasn't been taught to him?"

➤ Children of different ages must be assigned chores depending upon their ability to perform the same. They must start simple and become more complex as the child grows older.

➤ Confrontation is typically not effective and teaches your child behaviors that you most likely do not want them to display with you or with others.

➤ Ignoring children's negative behaviors or responding inappropriately may teach them that aggression works.

➢ We all need to teach our children to learn to love the truth and not be fearful of it and thus hide it!

➢ Parents have a huge responsibility to ensure that their children grow up to be valued individuals of society.

➢ Learning about the right and wrong actions early in life will help your children be good citizens.

➢ Kids always model parent behaviors: thus, if you want them to monitor their language, you must monitor yours.

➢ Educate your children about the power of language and its effect on the people around them.

➢ If you successfully impart to your child the basic behaviors expected of him when at public places, you can surely make every trip an enjoyable and learning experience!

Section 6: Fatherhood

Dads and Children

Whenever I have my "parenting workshops," I have undoubtedly found the ratio of mothers to fathers being fifty to two! Somehow, many cultures still emphasize the mother's role in bringing up children significantly. Society tells men that their primary role in the family is to bring in the paycheck. It is time to challenge this thought process and understand the father's role in a child's life and how vital this role is to the child's overall development.

Chris is a well-established CEO of a company. His son Keith is having academic and behavioral problems. Being a good father, Chris took Keith to the best child psychologist in town. After two sessions with Keith, the psychologist requested to meet with Chris alone. Chris was expecting a long-drawn-out perceptive diagnosis, but the following few sentences left him astonished. The psychologist remarked that Keith's only desire was for his dad to spend more time with him. Once his surprise settled down, Chris realized he needed to make more time to spend with Keith, which would mean altering his current lifestyle. Chris made those changes which resulted in changes in Keith's behavior. Chris's involvement in his son's life was also a major contributing factor to Keith's academic success.

Research indicates a father's absence in a child's life can result in low self-esteem, poor school performance, anti-social behavior, a higher incidence of depression, and a reduced ability to make positive peer relations.

Following is a list of activities to help dads become more involved in their child's life:

- Block out time when you come back home from work to spend with your children. Spend that time bonding with them, ask them about school, friends, or just play a game, anything that helps you all connect.

- Children need hugs to feel emotionally secure, do your part and hug your children. They will know you love them and care about them with this simple gesture.

- Involve yourself in little activities like bathing your children, reading them a bedtime story, or helping them with their homework.

- Attend your child's school functions and parent-teacher meetings so your child feels you are involved with his life.

- Make sure you plan outings with the family on the weekends. Take along some of your child's friends, so you can get to know them.

- If you must be away on business, write letters (yes, handwrite!) or emails to your children, so they feel connected. Letter's children receive from their parents are valued possessions that help strengthen parent/child relationships.

- Try to let go of your "quick-fix thinking." Spend time listening to your children. Generally, one of a dad's significant roles is to solve the problem; however, sometimes, children just need to be heard.

- You must closely monitor your children's development and provide support accordingly. Your children will require different degrees of understanding and care as they go through various growth and development stages.

- Spend time with your children, teaching them how they can strengthen their talents. This will help enhance their self-confidence.

- Decide with your partner on discipline rules so that there is consistency in what you both expect your children to follow. The absence of this makes it easy for children to take advantage of and play parents against each other. Decide on clear expectations and limits for your children to follow.

- Try not to let mood swings brought home from work affect your interactions with your children. Our kids need us to be consistent—*predictable* in our moods and habits.

- Give your children unconditional love and praise them for their ideas and accomplishments.

Remember when you first held your baby in your hands and felt overwhelmed with the feeling of "now what do I do?" With that feeling of anxiety, you handed over the especially important job of bringing up your child into the safe and competent hands of your partner. However, it is time to change that and start doing your part. Your little darlings need your care and support as much as their mothers to develop into well-balanced, complete human beings.

After all, at the end of your life, you will not be thinking about your achievements on the golf course, the largest fish you caught, your career growth chart, or even your stock portfolio. You will be wondering what you could have done differently with your kids.

In the words of Senator Sam Brownback, "If you ask children what they want, their answer is clear and unequivocal. They want their **mom and dad** to be around to give them love, time, and attention. To share both quality time and large quantities of time".

Dad – A Daughter's Hero

Recently, we conducted a workshop on "Understanding your Adolescent" for parents of teenagers. Our guest speaker for the evening, a renowned psychologist, covered all the topics relating to understanding teenagers very competently. One issue raised by more than one parent was the role a father plays in his daughter's life. The relationship between a dad and his daughter conjures up a combination of the warmest, most special emotions and feelings of sweetness and love.

However, many fathers take a back seat during adolescence because they are unsure how to deal with their girl's emotional and physical changes. Dads find it challenging to understand their growing girls since all they know is how they grew up to be a man. They are not sure of how it is to be a girl! Nevertheless, one of the most important things a dad can teach his daughter is just that…the differences between boys and girls.

For teenage boys, life is full of uncertainty and confusion about girls, the mystery and excitement about falling in love, moments of embarrassment or courage, and touching memories. Dads must share these memories and tell stories to their daughters because it gives daughters valuable insight into the world of boys and relationships. This is a perspective nobody else can share quite the way a father can.

What dads need to remember is

the most important gift you could give your daughter is listening.

You need to take what your girls feel and say seriously; if you do not do that, they feel invalidated. Too many times, dads want to quickly "fix" problems. If your little girl is in pain, "fixing" things may seem like a logical thing to want to do, but that can work against what you are trying to achieve. You want to build trust and openness in the relationship, support her, and help her grow. In situations when your daughters are upset, ask them what they want from you. Do they want you just to listen, or are they asking for your advice?

What dad says and how he acts will many times dictate how she ends up feeling about herself. From Dad, little girls gain their first reflection of themselves as a female. They develop a sense of acceptance or non-acceptance; they feel valued or discounted. When fathers are authoritative, rigidly set rules, are excessively critical, and all-powerful, girls find it difficult to build healthy self-esteem.

If a father is fair and listens to his daughter's thoughts,

she will gain self-confidence and pride in her own opinion.

When daughters learn to communicate with their fathers and trust that their opinion will count, girls can develop self-assuredness. This will allow them to be assertive and stand up for themselves.

Daughters learn about relationships from watching Mom and Dad. If parents treat each other well, this becomes a daughter's expectation from her relationships. However, if Dad is a dictator, then men are regarded as essentially controlling. If he is an alcoholic or is abusive, it reflects that men are permitted to get out of control and be hurtful. This could mean your daughter would accept this behavior in her relationships.

Fathers have a big responsibility to ensure a healthy self-image in their daughter and help her build and maintain meaningful relationships in her life.

136

Some of the most meaningful moments in a daughter's life are spent with her darling daddy. Fathers must make a conscious effort to be effective parents and experience the natural fruits of this wonderful relationship.

My Daddy

My daddy is the greatest daddy of them all,

And my daddy always won the game when he played ball.

And did I ever tell you how he caught a whale,

He dived into the ocean and grabbed it by its tail.

My daddy is the strongest man throughout the land,

And my daddy could beat Mohammad Ali with one hand.

My daddy was a C.B.I man, so he claims,

And my daddy could have shot it out with any criminal you can name.

They take him for Clooney; he is handsome, you see

And just to prove it…look at me!

-By a ten-year-old-girl

"It takes a man to make a son, but it takes a father to make a daughter," someone recently told me. We were discussing the influence of fathers in the lives of their daughters. I think these words perfectly summarized the essence of this significant relationship.

Another father who overheard us talking came up and said, "I don't know how to connect with my daughter. I wish I could, but I just cannot seem to establish that bond. I try to give her solutions to her problems when she decides to share them with me, but there is nothing else we have in common in what we like to do! She loves her dolls, and I cannot see myself spending too much time with that. She loves braiding her hair, and that is not something that I think I should get involved in doing. I am just lost in trying to connect."

Another father remarked sadly, "I think fathers are the icing on the cake." Since his wife was so important to his daughter, he felt that his need was just like the icing!

So, why should fathers want to connect with their daughters, and how should they accomplish it?

Well, to begin with, fathers must know that they are particularly essential to their daughters. Daughters need their fathers to encourage their talents and affirm their femininity. They need to know that the first man in their life is head over heels in love with them so that they grow up with confidence and high self-worth.

A father needs to discover his daughter in ways different from understanding his son. The first and, I guess, an essential way for a father to connect with his daughter is to listen to her.

"My father is my role model. I compare all the other men in the world to him. My dad is the most loving, tolerant, admirable, dependable man I have ever known. He is the model that I judge all other men by. Sharing this kind of relationship with my dad has given me a lot of faith, encouragement, and direction. The love and support I have had through the years, and continue to have, has made me a much stronger person," recalled a client of mine.

Most girls look up to their fathers as their heroes. A father's behavior towards his daughter dictates how she would end up feeling about herself. An overly critical and rigid, and authoritative father would make it extremely difficult for his daughter to grow up with healthy self-esteem. On the other hand, if a father shares a warm, trusting relationship with his daughter, she is more likely to grow up to be a self-assured and assertive person.

The first male relationship a girl has is with her father, which will dictate all subsequent relationships with men. Fathers can either send their daughters down life's roads with clear and healthy expectations of men or leave them confused and shaky about what to accept in their relationships. It is a father's responsibility to ensure that his daughter wanders into the world of men with an example of a strong, nurturing, and supportive masculinity.

Fathers also have a significant influence on the academic and career-related success of their daughters.

Healthy father/daughter relationships ensure independence and competence, the key elements to navigating the world outside the home.,

When I have asked, daughters say they wanted their dads to spend more time with them, communicate better, and understand their aspirations and likes. Fathering a daughter is tough, and many find it easier to give up and leave the upbringing to the mothers. However, your daughter needs you just as much as she needs her mother to help her successfully steer the passage from girl to woman.

Today, tell your daughter how beautiful you think she is, how proud you are of her achievements, and everything she has become. Tell her how incredibly special she is to you and see her face light up! The pride beaming on her face because her dad, her hero, thinks she is special will make this tough challenge of fathering a daughter all worth it.

Key Points

➢ Research indicates that father absence in a child's life can lead to low self-esteem, poor school performance, anti-social behavior, a higher incidence of depression, and reduced ability to make positive peer relations.

➢ Spend time listening to your children.

➢ Give your children unconditional love and praise them for their ideas and accomplishments rather than constantly disciplining them and pointing out their faults.

➢ What dads need to remember is that the most important gift you could give your daughters is **listening**.

➢ If a father is fair and listens to his daughter's thoughts, she will gain self-confidence and pride in her own opinion.

➢ Fathers have a big responsibility of ensuring a healthy self-image in their daughters and helping her build and maintain meaningful relationships in her life.

➤ Healthy father/daughter relationships ensure independence and competence, the key elements to navigating the world outside the home.

Section 7: Tweens and Teens

Making Your Home Environment Pre-Teen Friendly

The pre-teen years are challenging ones for kids and parents. As a therapist, I help adolescents daily with these age-related struggles and challenges. The good news is that most kids do make it through adolescence with little or no permanent scars. However, not without the love and support from their parents. Here are some basics for parents to keep in mind for creating a home environment that is both safe and engaging for their tweens.

Some tweens, particularly boys, are not used to being open to discussing their lives. Parents must ask their kids to tell them about what they did in and after school. You must ask for and validate your child's opinions. Sometimes, it helps to begin a conversation with a topic that is sure to be of interest to your child, such as fashion, sports, or music. Another idea is to plan at least one activity a month with your child of his choosing where talking, and listening can occur, perhaps at the mall or bowling alley.

Parents need to talk to their kids about the dangers of essential issues such as smoking, drugs, and alcohol. It can be harmful to assume they have all the facts and understand the consequences of experimentation. In middle school, your children are likely exposed to and will be forced to make choices with potentially serious consequences. It is only natural that pre-teens will make some mistakes on their own. Parents need to let their kids know they are there for them and come to them no matter what problem they may be experiencing. Even kids from the most stable homes need to be reminded of this.

Parents are overly concerned with making a safe physical surrounding for infants, toddlers, and preschoolers during the early years of childhood. As children grow and their needs change, we must remind ourselves that our goals remain the same, that is, to keep our kids safe and thriving. We want them to do their best and avoid what is potentially harmful to them. Children of all ages need boundaries and guidance. Open and continuous communication, as well as a safe and engaging home life, will help ensure growth and happiness for your tween!

Hey Mom… Don't I Look Cool!

"How come I don't look like the girls in the fashion magazines? It's not like I don't try! I try to dress like them, wear make-up, and even style my hair like them. What's wrong with me?" exclaimed Tanya to me during one of our initial meetings.

Most teens spend a lot of time agonizing about their looks. They would do whatever it takes to look cool.

Parents often face trouble when their teens over-use makeup or dress in an unacceptable fashion for the family. Teenagers need guidelines, and parents need to be open about which grooming behaviors they will accept. Make agreements with your children about acceptable dressing and emphasize the importance of keeping these agreements.

Developing and then following a set of agreements is one way to keep a relationship healthy.

When confronting your teen, there are four keys to remember about the need for change in some aspect of his behavior and making agreements: Empathy, Courtesy, Brevity, and Timing.

One of the best ways for parents to communicate with their teens is by making statements that reflect a sincere awareness of their feelings. Being empathetic means putting yourself in the other person's shoes. Parents tend to forget their teen days and the fact that many of them might have had parents who objected to their dress or grooming choices. Now it is your turn to play the guiding role. You must give the message "I care" to your kids and ensure they know that you only want what is best for them. If your teens engage in improper grooming behavior, parents can calmly say, "I love you very much, and that's why I feel I have to say something you may not want to hear. I hope you can see that your make-up or dress is unacceptable, so I am asking you to change. You have good judgment, and I am confident that you will realize that I am only asking you to do this because I love you and want what's best for you."

Basic personal courtesy is fundamental when confronting teens. Never start by accusing your teen of doing something wrong. Make your conversation friendly, not hostile. Many parents make remarks like, "You dress so shabby," comments like these will not improve the child's appearance. Yelling or screaming or calling names will only make it difficult to get the message across to your teen.

Convey trust in your teens and confidence in their judgment and abilities. This will make them feel more responsible and rethink their decisions. State your concerns in a few words. Words used to direct your teen are like tires. The more time a tire goes around, the more tread it loses and the less efficient it becomes. In the same way, the longer you go on, the less impactful you will be. Your teen will gradually become used to the words, and you might feel the need to raise your voice or combine your words with threats to get your message across. These tactics fail to achieve the purpose and instead trigger a more intense desire in your teen to do the very thing for which she is being reprimanded.

Timing is vital for your teen's sake as well as your own. Be sensitive about where and when to confront them. Matters of dressing and grooming may embarrass them in front of relatives and friends. These matters need to be discussed in private. Avoid hurtful messages when your teen is already upset, angry, or sad. Another time to avoid confrontation is when you are under stress, tired, or are feeling overwhelmed. Calm yourself down first and then broach the matter.

Often, teens do not meet their parents' expectations because they are unreasonable. Rules should be made in tune with what they ready for. Putting pressure on your teens to conform entirely to your taste without giving a thought to their likes, dislikes, or current trends is likely to cause frustration and a strained relationship between you and your teen. Remember, by setting unrealistic rules for grooming, you are forcing your teens to rebel.

Parents must perform the tricky balancing act of encouraging their teens to become independent while at the same time guiding them when needed. Your teen's dress and grooming are crucial concerns and often a cause of conflict in the home. If dealt with properly, this issue can be tackled without upsetting your teen or compromising family values.

Support Your Youngsters

Rewind to your pre-teen or tween years for a moment. Recall the emotional turmoil you went through sitting on the fence between childhood and adulthood. Remember how you wanted your parent's support and approval yet expected them to know when to back off instinctively?

Now you are the parent, and although you are not new at this, there are probably moments when you are as confused as your teens in dealing with their emotions and behaviors. Your sweet angels of yesterday begin to act like you are their worst enemy. Things like the phone become their personal domain, and bribing, or a dire emergency is the only way to get it out of their grasp.

As a counselor, I talk to parents each day seeking ways to get to know their teens better and guide them appropriately. Claudia, a mother of a fifteen-year-old, expressed to me, "I don't know what's come over my daughter. She is always arguing with me about silly things. Not a single day goes by without her screaming and storming out of the room. I don't know how to deal with her." So, what are parents to do when their children suddenly act so differently?

One of the most important factors that helps an adolescent deal with this turbulent time is unconditional love and consistent support from a parent. You must also model appropriate behavior, communicate with your teens, and know all about their world. This is the time when teenagers try to assert their individuality. This is not the time to play the great dictator and alienate your teens. Now is when they need your love and care the most. The kind of support you give your teens at this stage will determine the type of individuals they grow up to be.

Model Your Behavior: From the beginning of their lives, children imitate their parents. Parental example is one of the best teaching tools we have. Parents who value people, the law, education, and honesty will most likely have teens who value the same. Parents play a significant role in developing a teen's value system. Modeling appropriate behavior is probably 90 percent of parenting. Adolescents who feel good about themselves and their home life will be far less likely to turn to negative influences.

Communicate with Your Kids: Listen to your teens without judging them. Try to see their point of view even if you disagree with them. Validate their feelings. Let them know that it is okay to be angry or confused. Guide your teens towards appropriate anger-releasing outlets such as exercise, talking, or writing in a journal. Establish the rules such as bedtime and curfew right in the beginning and live by any consequences you set. You must follow some rules yourself if you want your children to do the same. Things like spending less time on the phone, watching television, and putting things away must be rules that everyone in the family is expected to follow.

Parents sometimes forget that they were teenagers too, and their self-righteousness does not win them any points with their teens. Calmly speak to your teen even if you are upset. Request instead of demanding. Ask instead of telling. Make agreements instead of dictating rules. Involve them in decision-making instead of deciding for them. Accept that their priorities and perspectives may be completely different from yours.

Getting the message, we are in this together across to your teenagers will help build a respectful and cooperative relationship with them.

Know Your Teens: I always tell parents that they are at a loss if they do not know what is happening in their teen's life. It is when you know their world that you can guide and help your teens. You must know how, and with whom your teens spend their time when they are not with you. Talk to them about their interests, school, and friends. Make certain parties that they attend are appropriately chaperoned. Let your teens know what you do not approve of them doing, such as smoking and drinking, while explaining the consequences of such acts.

It is encouraging when a parent tells me that he shares such a close relationship with his teenager and is confident she would tell him whatever trouble she got into. These parents always know what is going on in their child's life and can guide and support her.

Parenting is a balancing act from the start. Providing a positive example, communicating daily, and knowing your kids as individuals can help your child succeed and be happy during these challenging years. Parents are a significant influence in their teens' lives. Give your teens unconditional love, understanding, and guidance, and enjoy them!

Leaving the Nest

While they are in the trenches, parents often think nothing will be worse than the "terrible twos" or the pre-teen years. However, many discover one of the biggest parenting challenges is when their children are getting ready to leave the nest to go to college. One-part independent adult and one-part scared child, teenagers need lots of parenting support to make this critical transition. Parents play a significant role in helping their children who are heading to college be well prepared.

Sana, a second-year student at Boston University, USA, says, "Probably the most important thing that my parents did for me was to be there for me to talk to about my fears, ideas, and hopes. The support they provided me was a pillar of strength throughout the rough transition period from school to university and home to dorm."

Teens who are prepared to handle personal freedom and responsibility can adjust very well to the college environment. A vast majority of college student's problems, including poor academic performance and concerns outside the classroom, boil down to personal responsibility issues and making good decisions or handling the newfound freedom. For instance, students must decide whether to go to class or blow it off to be with friends, get enough sleep or party all night, and eat right or live on junk food.

To help kids meet the challenges that their college life has to offer, parents need to talk to them about several issues, such as family values, the importance of academic success, choosing the right friends, and coping with the loss of the familiar home and school structure. Talk to your teens about the benefits of healthy habits, such as exercising and time-management techniques to help them manage their time effectively. Studies show that poor use of time is the biggest single reason students fail academically. Students in college must also deal with the additional responsibility of managing their money. Parents can help by teaching their teens money management.

You must help your kids understand the essence of a successful student is in making good friends, getting good grades, and becoming involved socially. Teach your kids that academic success depends entirely on focus. Procrastinating or making excuses might work in high school but not in college. Also, encourage your child to join clubs or volunteer for high school activities to develop their social skills. Such actions will require them to meet new people, talk about themselves, ask questions, be assertive, and get involved. These skills help teenagers meet people and make friends in the new environment. It teaches them to adjust to people who are different from them and have different value systems.

Parents need to discuss communication channels with their kids, such as weekly e-mails and phone calls. Ensure that your teens come home during breaks for the first few semesters. Open communication allows families to help their children through the difficult transition by building a supportive structure.

Moving to college is a big adjustment, especially if your child has gone to a single-gender high school or has had a very nurturing and conservative environment at home and school. You must talk to your kids about the importance of saying "No." Many times, dangerous habits are developed due to peer pressure. Your teens need to know that it is okay to leave a situation when they do not feel safe or comfortable. They need to be told that there are enough people in the college and find individuals who fit their style. Harry, a student at the University of Virginia, said, "The most valuable piece of advice I got from my parents was to always be myself. I learned to live by my standards, which helped me during the difficult transition."

Your kids must understand that they are in charge now, and every decision they make will affect their lives somehow. They also need to be taught to forgive themselves, learn from their mistakes, and move on if they make some wrong decisions.

Talking to someone who has recently started his college life will help your child immensely. Getting information on the activities, dorm life, other housing options, and the college culture can help him get acquainted with and be prepared for the college environment.

College-bound youngsters slip into all sorts of roles. Some seem so excited about leaving for college, while others can barely stand it. The summer before independence can be the most insecure summer of a young person's life. Ultimately, how much parents prepare their kids for life after high school helps determine their college success. Although you are not going to be around physically, your support is invaluable.

Parents need to talk to their teens about coping strategies, about accepting their feelings, about why it is okay to make mistakes, and most importantly, about how you will always be there for them.

Life Skills for Your Teens

"When I went away to college, suddenly, I was 'in charge' of everything, from groceries to laundry, cooking, and cleaning. The first few weeks were a nightmare. Away from the protected life I had lived with my parents; I was in this strange land fending for all my needs. The worst part was I was unprepared for what life demanded of me there. I did not have the necessary skills that would help me survive the ordeal that I faced!" reported Tony, one of my students who was pursuing his higher education abroad.

Life skills are essentially those that help promote mental well-being and competence in young people as they face life's realities.

Many students who go away to study find themselves in situations of distress like those faced by Tony. Thus, it is vital to teach our children some essential life skills that will save them a lot of trouble when they go to college.

The following are some skills I feel would help children better deal with life away from home:

- The first and most crucial skill to equip our children with is cooking. We do not need to make our children expert chefs; however, we need to ensure that they have basic survival cooking skills. Teach them how to read and follow basic recipes. Make sure they know how to use the Microwave oven, toaster oven, blender, and mixer. Also, ensure they understand the basic cooking vocabulary, including chop, dice, sauté, mince, and grate.
- Next in line is to teach your children how to do their laundry. Kids must know how to operate a washing machine and dryer. Show your kids the mechanics of using these machines like the right temperature, separate the color and black and white clothes, and the ideal amount of a load.

- Educate your kids about shopping for their groceries. Teach them about value-buying so they do not end up spending too much unnecessarily.

- Opening a bank account and handling a checkbook are again essential skills your children need to be taught. Talk to your children about the importance of saving and maintaining a good credit history. Also, teach them about checking the monthly bank statements.

- Train your children on how to write a good resume and appropriate interviewing skills. You can get information about these topics from several websites and college and career counselors. These skills are essential when your children apply for on-campus jobs or internships.

- Teach your children to pay bills on time and budget their expenses. This will help them in becoming responsible consumers. Many students get into debt because of a lack of these skills, which results in a bad credit standing.

- Educate your kids about car maintenance. Teach them how to check fluid levels in their car and talk to them about regular servicing.

It may seem as if these things are basic, and you might feel your children should know these skills by now, but you will be surprised how many do not.

Teaching your children about handling money, banking, shopping, and cooking

155

is the best way you can equip them when they are about to embark upon the journey

of attaining their education while saving them a tremendous amount of anguish.

Endowing them with these skills will give them a great head start to their future!

Helping Children Make Career Choices

From aerospace engineer to a microbiologist to an accountant to a fashion designer, the sky's the limit in choosing a career. Children need guidance to select the best career path. In making their choices, young people need to have a good understanding of themselves and their abilities. They must explore many different careers, thinking about what they like and dislike each before focusing on a particular path. It is imperative to have a career plan before investing time, energy, and money in college.

Parents have a strong influence on their children's decisions about education and careers. Parents know their child better than anyone else and have more interest in helping their child choose a rewarding career. Thus, you must take an active part in your child's decision about their future career. The first step to doing this is to help your child identify his or her interests, skills, and values. This can be done by talking to your child about his or her likes and dislikes and how these may relate to certain career choices. An interest in the outdoors could lead to careers ranging from gardening to oceanography.

Another way to do this is by contacting your child's school counselor for a formal assessment of interests and skills. The next step is to learn about the different careers you have identified through formal evaluations or discussions with your child. You can help your child collect information from the Internet and books. Your child can also talk to people in those fields and ask them questions about what they do in a typical day, why they decided on that career, what kind of training they needed for this career, and what they like most and least about their work.

It would also be beneficial if you can arrange for your child to get some work experience in the fields of their interest. Volunteer work and part-time employment are great ways to learn about jobs. Remember, helping your child understand that something may not be suitable for them is just as important as finding something of interest. Many of us have heard more than one story of a student who wants to be a teacher, only to reach the classroom and realize that they do not have the temperament for handling children. Having them exposed to a career first could save so much time, money, and effort.

Another way of getting career-related information is at Career Fairs. These fairs attract people from a range of fields and jobs available to talk to about their work and what kind of education and training is needed for that work. You can attend career fairs with your child and talk about the various careers represented. There is a wealth of other information on the web that describes occupations, salaries, projections for the future, and other trends. This is a crucial point to consider before helping your child to decide on a career path.

After choosing the right career, your child then must chalk out the right educational plan to help her get there. For example, a degree in counseling would require your child to earn a bachelor's degree in psychology and a master's degree in counseling or mental health. You can help your child research the colleges and courses available to them to pursue their higher education.

Over time, many factors influence your child's career development process. These include education, dreams, role models, values, family, spiritual beliefs, testing, guidance, leisure and recreation activities, lifestyles, and unhappy experiences.

Remember, knowing who they are and what will make them happy are critical steps in your children's career development process.

Be open to different definitions for success. Success is not all about money or advanced degrees. It is about loving the job and being able to make a difference in the work environment. Remember that a career choice is a personal decision.

Do not make your children live your dreams.

Make career decisions with and not for your child.

Mom, Dad... I'm Off to Work!

Jessica and Sam were repeatedly in my office before the summer holidays to find out how they could get a job over the summer. Both had different reasons for why they wanted to join the workforce. For Jessica, it was more about passing her time productively for the two hot months, while Sam was trying to earn some money to not be dependent on his parents for every little need.

Encouraging your children to hold part-time jobs can be both helpful and hurtful to them. Kids view getting a job to make extra cash, get out of the house, interact with others their age, and feel grown-up.

As parents, your considerations about your kids taking on part-time jobs should include what they will learn from the experience and the real-life situations they will be entering. You can use their desire to enter the workforce as an opportunity to further their financial and budgeting education. You may want to help them develop a budget and encourage them to open a savings and checking account if they do not have one already.

Working also helps teach your children other essential qualities like tolerance, empathy, patience, and teamwork. These traits will help your children go a long way in their life and in the careers they choose. Holding jobs and gaining experience can also help your teens have an edge when applying to universities. One fundamental matter is that you still must make sure they are doing their schoolwork in a timely and daily fashion. Make sure your teen understands that if grades begin to decline, he or she will be expected to cut work hours.

A good rule of thumb is to require that your children work less than twenty hours a week at their job. Any more than this, and it starts interfering with their schoolwork, typically. That set number of hours each week helps them earn plenty of extra income and gain a sense of independence and achievement. If possible, part-time work should be limited to weekends.

For many teenagers, holding a part-time job is an essential rite of passage into adulthood. It teaches them about the world, life skills, and how to manage money. Through these, teenagers understand what it takes to become successful adults in society and see how the world works.

If it does not interfere with their education,

Part-time jobs can help with the overall development of your teen!

Teen Effective Parenting

Ted's mom had tears in her eyes as she expressed her concerns regarding Ted's behaviors. He is seventeen years old and lacks a total sense of responsibility. He spends hours on the Internet and phone. He does not want to study and is out late every night. His mom is also concerned Ted may be drinking and smoking when he is out with his friends. She does not know how to stop him or make him understand the harm he is causing to himself and the family.

During the teen years, parenting can be incredibly challenging. Parents need to draw the line between being involved in their child's life yet ensuring the freedom and space he needs. However, parents need to bear in mind their teens count on them for their guidance and support. One of the most challenging aspects of setting limits for your child is drawing the line between too much and too little. Parents must be vigilant enough to set rules and expect them to be followed. It is also vital that parents provide consequences if the rules are broken. Although sometimes discipline is not pleasant, it can help save the whole family heartaches in the future.

Clear boundaries and standards provide teens the much-needed stability to handle relationships, roles and establish their own identities.

The first step to understanding your teen is listening to him. Ask your teen how his day was and listen to all the details so that he knows you are interested. Ask if he needs help dealing with any issues. Ask about his friends and classes. You need to listen without judging. Understanding your teen's life is the first step and a particularly significant one for you to guide him.

Adolescents usually demand freedom. It is essential for parents to understand this need, but not without communicating this privilege must be earned by displaying adequate responsibility. For example, if your son's curfew is 11 p.m. and he chooses not to respect that, maybe you will have to reconsider this freedom. Too permissive parenting has often been associated with behavior problems.

Teens need appropriate boundaries and limits. The most effective way is to involve them in setting up the rules because they are more likely to follow through. Check-in with your teen's school staff periodically to understand how they are performing at school. Know your teen's friends because they are an important part of their life and most often have a significant influence. Peer pressure can make children resort to acting in ways they later grow to regret. Thus, being a part of their world of friends is essential. Also, parents need to allow for independent thought and expression to raise children with a healthy sense of self who make the right decisions, withstanding peer pressure.

Joshua's dad was shocked when he caught his son smoking. He was only thirteen. Dad is a smoker himself but never thought his son would want to follow so young. Parents forget that their behavior is an example for their children. You are your child's first role model; thus, it is vital to monitor your behaviors.

Often parents have found that spending time engaging in recreational activities with your teen is the best way to connect. Regular and positive interaction is important for monitoring your teen and their activities. When the relationship between children and parents is characterized by warmth and kindness, it is easier to implement discipline rules, and they are more likely to be followed.

Attempting to control your child's behavior by using guilt, withdrawing love,

or invalidating feelings or beliefs is futile in the long run.

Instead, if the parent tries to offer explanations and interpretations of the event along with understanding and respecting the interpretations of the child, they are more likely to follow through without the damaging effects of psychological control.

To effectively guide your teen into becoming a healthy and well-balanced adult member of society, you must invest time and energy. Inculcating the correct values and ideas will see you through this exciting and adventurous journey from childhood to adulthood. Parents who share a warm, kind, and solid relationship with their child, display respect for his ideas, take an active interest in their child's activities, and set firm boundaries for those activities will surely deter the challenging bumps on the way.

Riding Emotional Waves

Emotions come and go like waves. Sometimes you feel intensely angry, sad, or scared. Other times, you feel exceedingly happy, embarrassed, or confused. This is true for everyone, but especially for teens, whose emotional swings can be frequent and dramatic. A mother of a fourteen-year-old explains that she cannot understand or predict her daughter's behavior.

"One day, she is all smiles and so angelic, and the other, she behaves like the demon from hell. A single day does not go by without her screaming at me and storming out of the room," exclaimed this mother.

Hormones and events in our lives trigger emotions. We cannot necessarily choose our emotions or prevent them. We can, however, choose to express these feelings in healthy ways. You cannot control waves, but you can learn to ride them, stay afloat, and not get dragged down by the undertow.

An essential part of parenting is to teach our teens

to identify, accept, and express their feelings in positive ways.

When families communicate well and work cooperatively, intense emotions can be handled without a problem. However, when managed poorly, these emotions get in the way of good communication between parent and child.

164

According to one father, "My teenage son doesn't know how to handle his intense feelings. He talks back to us and even swears at us. He does not do what we ask him to do. He seems to be trying to aggravate us. I feel like things are out of control."

Our teens need to learn how not to direct their emotional outbursts at others or turn them inward where it eats away at them. Instead, they should deal with them in constructive ways. Depending upon their mood, it may not take much to make your teens mad.

For many youngsters, dealing with intense emotions means yelling, slamming doors, and throwing things. If any of this sounds familiar, you know that your teens are not positively coping with their anger.

Ask your teens to follow these steps to help them manage their emotions:

- Request your teen to walk away from a situation that might be causing distress. Before they can resolve the situation, they must gain control of themselves. Explain to them that they should spend some time alone and find a quiet place to think.
- Encourage them to calm down by doing some grounding exercises. Deep breathing will slow down their racing heart. Exercising also helps to calm down. Ask your teens to run around the block or dance to some music to clear their minds and get some perspective on what happened. Journaling is another highly effective tool to help your teen calm down.
- Next, your teen could reflect upon the situation. Ask them to think about the following questions: What did I do that added to the

situation deteriorating? What can I do to keep it from happening again?

- Assist your teen in looking at another person's point of view. Ask them, "If you were that person, how would you have acted or reacted?" Help them build empathy for others.

Most adolescents feel they are on an emotional rollercoaster, one minute up and down the next. Teenagers are a mass of confusion as they sit on the fence between childhood and adulthood. With the many changes that occur during adolescence, it is not unusual for teenagers to experience intense emotions. Adolescents struggle to establish and prepare for adulthood. Sometimes emotional outbursts are their way of asserting independence.

The tumultuous teenage years are when our patience and endurance as parents are put to the ultimate test. Remember, your kids will always model your behavior. Dealing appropriately when you are angry will help ensure your teens will follow. Parents can be good role models and open the door to constructive communication with their children.

Let your teen know that they may not have a choice in feeling what they feel, but they have a choice in how to respond to and address those feelings. Help them become aware of the warning signs of their outburst and teach them ways to deal with this emotional rollercoaster!

Puberty and Girls

Veronica and Natasha were two well-adjusted, happy, and successful fourth graders. Veronica excelled in all her subjects in school and particularly enjoyed Science and Math. Her face lit up whenever she talked about her dream of becoming a pilot. Natasha was described by her teachers as a "sweet, quiet girl" who was always willing to help her teachers and classmates. She wanted to grow up to be a nurse and help people. Teachers were confident that these two girls would have no difficulty achieving academic, career, and personal success as they matured.

Despite the teacher's predictions, a look at these girls just a few years later revealed a vastly different picture. By the time she was fourteen years old, Veronica's grades had dropped significantly. She appeared withdrawn, and her parents and teachers felt that they could not reach her. The same girl who had once excelled now seemed to have lost her motivation and self-confidence. She no longer spoke of her career aspirations. Her academic performance saw a significant decline. She had also developed an eating disorder as a means of coping. At fifteen years of age, Natasha, who had always been noted for her caring nature, was consistently getting into trouble for bullying and fighting with other girls. She was furious and hostile at home.

The changes witnessed in these two girls are not uncommon. Researchers have noted a psychological shift that occurs as girls move from childhood to adolescence. Whereas during the first decade of life, girls typically exhibit self-confidence, vitality, and a sense of mastery in

167

many areas. The second decade is often accompanied by self-doubt and inhibition.

Studies have revealed that upon entering adolescence, girls experience sudden and dramatic declines in self-esteem. Girls entering puberty often face a "crisis in confidence," which makes them vulnerable to risky behavior. These bad choices can have devastating lifelong consequences.

Life often becomes confusing for young girls as they struggle to negotiate the conflicting demands of self and society. As they embark on the journey to womanhood, girls become aware of their female identity and the expectations that society has of women. When societal experiences and expectations conflict with girls' needs, ambition, and self-perceptions, they experience a psychological crisis. In the face of such a crisis, girls may attempt to cope with the situation in self-defeating ways. Like Veronica, they may become depressed or withdrawn, or, like Natasha, may display anger and aggression against herself and others.

As parents, we have complex emotional relationships with our daughters. Parents can take the following steps to help their teenage girls successfully navigate the journey to adulthood.

To help girls develop into healthy, confident, and successful young women, we must start by examining our own gender biases. It is crucial to know although we have the best intentions, we may still manifest gender biases that can unconsciously affect interactions with our daughters.

Help build your daughter's self-esteem by letting her know that you trust her and her decisions. Avoid the temptation to offer advice constantly; encourage girls to think for themselves. If your daughter expresses self-doubt about her abilities, encourage her to examine the validity of her belief objectively. Explore and encourage your daughter to pursue her talents.

It is imperative to tell your daughter that you love her, and no matter what happens, you will always care for her. Be there when she needs you. Do not ever give up on her. With your love and support, your daughter can pass the tests of life and be able to tackle hurdles with courage.

Try to empower your girls by helping them deal with feelings of inner conflicts that lead them to self-destructive coping mechanisms such as eating disorders and self-injury. To help girls through this difficult phase, we must acknowledge the realities they face, trust them with their decisions, and not place too many limits or expectations on their life choices.

If they know we believe in them, girls will begin to believe in themselves.

They will become strong, confident, and successful women.

Helping Teens Deal with Stress

Today's adolescents are stressed about a lot of issues. "What am I going to do in life? Who are my true friends? What do I do about my failing grades? How should I deal with peer pressure? How am I ever going to live up to my parents' expectations?" It is important to remember stress is a natural part of your child's life. It only becomes harmful when the problems and hassles of daily life overwhelm your child. Parents must support their children to cope better with this overly complex phase of their lives.

Some symptoms parents need to watch out for

that are indications of their child being excessively stressed include:

aggression, withdrawal, physical illness, sleeplessness, depression,

and drastic weight loss or gain.

In addition to affecting health, stress also affects a teenager's sense of well-being. They may get defensive, argumentative, or impatient in their interactions with people and become truant at school. Their ability to be loving toward others and to be tolerant of mistakes is diminished. They feel anxious and frustrated. They start making mistakes and having accidents. They lose their self-confidence and their sense of self.

So, what can parents do to be more supportive?

First, it is essential to keep the channels of communication open between you and your teen. If your child is not comfortable talking to you about her worries, there will be little you will be able to do to help her. Most often, all teens want is a listening ear and not someone to tell them what to do. This does not mean you should not express your opinions, particularly on crucial matters like values. But if every discussion turns into an argument, you may need to spend more time listening and express your views calmly.

In addition to open communication, your teen probably needs you to help them with scheduling. Sometimes they over-extend themselves. Some teenagers find themselves swamped when they add an after-school activity to an already full day or are expected to do too much at home. Although teenagers should be doing regular chores, some become overburdened with them. Make sure your teenager has enough time to relax. Also, help your teen learn to pace themselves, so they do not feel overwhelmed.

Another excellent way for your teenager to deal with stress is by encouraging them to get into physical activity of their choice. Swimming, jogging, cycling, or skating are all ways of releasing tension.

Teach your teen how to identify stressful situations and some coping strategies to help him deal with them. Use humor to buffer bad feelings and situations. A child who learns to use humor will be better able to keep things in perspective.

Make sure you do not criticize your teens. They already have a tough time trying to establish an identity, and your negative comments can make that process exceedingly tricky. Build your teenager's confidence and self-esteem by remembering to praise them when they do something good. With the foundation of confidence and self-esteem that you provide, your teenager will be better able to handle changes and stress.

Show your teenager how to focus on the positive aspects of a situation. Have him try and list the benefits and opportunities created rather than the problems. Even the most unpleasant experiences can lead to growth and outcomes.

Despite all your effort, sometimes adolescents find it is challenging to seek help from their families. When pressures become extreme, and solutions run out, it is time to talk about getting help.

When you see evidence that your child is highly stressed

and is resorting to maladaptive coping methods,

get professional help immediately.

Children cannot escape the stress and the pressures that come with living in today's world, but they can learn effective coping methods. Always model healthy coping behaviors and be there to back your teens. A little support at this time can go a long way to ensuring a healthy, well-balanced individual in the future!

Teen Depression

For generations, parents have been troubled by the moodiness of their teens. Today adolescence is an even more stressful and confusing time due to changing family patterns and too many expectations. Adolescents go through a period of uncertainty and zxacsdwfer34t5 as they try to find their ground and establish their independence. Everything seems in a state of flux–their moods, their bodies, and their relationships with family and friends. Most teenagers emerge unscarred or maybe with just a few nicks and bruises. But others just cannot cope with the tumult of emotions, and they fall into a deep depression.

Depression affects more teens than ever, and about half of all cases of teen depression are unrecognized and untreated.

If one or more of these signs of depression persist in your teens, you should immediately seek help:

- **Frequent sadness, tearfulness, crying**

Teens may display pervasive sadness and cry for no apparent reason. They may feel hopeless, that life is not worth living, believe that a negative situation will never change, and become pessimistic about their future.

- **Decreased interest in activities or inability to enjoy previously favorite activities**

Teens may become apathetic and drop out of clubs, sports, and other activities they once enjoyed. Not much seems fun anymore to the depressed teen. Lack of motivation and lowered energy level is also reflected in missed classes or not going to school. A drop in grade averages can be equated with loss of concentration and slowed thinking.

- **Social isolation, poor communication**

There is a lack of connection with friends and family. Teens may avoid family gatherings and events and may be seen spending most of their time alone and without interests. They may not share their feelings with others, believing that they are alone in the world and no one is listening to them or even cares about them.

- **Low self-esteem and guilt**

Teens may assume blame for adverse events or circumstances. They may feel like a failure and have negative views about their competence and self-worth. They feel as if they are not "good enough."

- **Increased irritability, anger, or hostility**

Depressed teens are often irritable, taking out most of their anger on their family. They may attack others by being critical, sarcastic, or abusive.

- **Frequent complaints of physical illnesses, such as headaches**

Teens may complain about lightheadedness or dizziness, nausea, and back pain. Other common complaints include headaches, stomachaches, and vomiting. There may also be a significant change in eating and sleeping behaviors.

- **Thoughts or expressions of suicide or self-destructive behavior**

Teens who are depressed may say they want to be dead or may talk about suicide. Depressed children and teens are at increased risk for engaging in self-destructive behavior.

Your teens are going through a period of intense changes and confusion. Depression can prevent them from enjoying and benefiting from these years altogether. If you feel that your child is suffering from depression, seek help from a mental health professional. In addition to individual and group therapy, mental health professionals may also recommend the use of medications to help treat teen depression.

One of the best things you as parents can do to help your teens

is communicate with them.

Let them know that you care for and love them. Help them feel accepted and understood and give them the strength to fight this state of mind, be happy and smile again!

Teens and Substance Abuse

Adolescence is a time for trying new things. Experimentation with alcohol, drugs, and cigarettes during adolescence is common. In my sessions with teenagers, they talk a lot about how and why they started drinking or vaping. Many of them start to get accepted by their peer groups or feel grown-up. Some of them do it to cope with stress, and still, others begin to satisfy their curiosity. Whatever the reason, teenagers fail to realize there is a fine line between when you do something occasionally and when it becomes an addiction. Unfortunately, teenagers often do not see the link between their actions today and the consequences tomorrow. Some teens will experiment and stop or continue to use occasionally without significant problems. Others will develop a dependency, moving on to more dangerous substances, causing substantial harm to themselves and possibly others.

Some teenagers are more likely than others to get attracted to and get hooked on addictive substances. The risk in teens increases with factors including a family history of alcohol, drugs, or smoking, family unrest, learning difficulties resulting in school failure, low self-esteem, behavior problems, and rebelliousness.

Some signs can help parents decide if a problem is looming or their child is already involved in substance use. Adolescence is a bumpy ride, and some of these warning signs may only be the typical signs of growing up, but parents must be alert to the possibility that, with their child, they may signal trouble.

In general, you should suspect some substance use if you observe one or more of these indicators:

- Fatigue, repeated health complaints, red and glazed eyes, and a lasting cough.
- A change of friends from those you know and new friends who seem to avoid you.
- A best friend who is involved in substance abuse is the single best indicator of use.
- Deterioration in appearance. Not taking care of their looks or overindulging in their looks to mask their abuse habits.
- A decline in performance at home. Chores may be neglected or done sloppily; curfews may be ignored.
- A change in school performance. The drop in grades may or may not be a dramatic sign by itself, but watch for tardiness, truancy, and disciplinary problems.

- Hypersensitivity, and irritability. The teenage user is often hostile, avoids family contact, overreacts to mild criticism, and deflects the topic when pressed for accountability.
- Wide mood swings. Although mood changes are a normal part of adolescence, extreme emotional swings indicate a problem and maybe the result of drug or alcohol use.
- The disappearance of money, personal belongings, cigarettes, or alcohol from the house.

If you feel that your teen is having problems with substances, the first thing to do is confront him about it and try to get to the root of the problem. Initially, be prepared for denial, defiance, and irrational behavior on the part of your teen. Do not play tyrant at this time because that might only backfire. Keep in mind that being judgmental and negative will only send your teen further into his shell.

If your child is not sharing with you and thus you are not able to do much to help, it would be appropriate to seek professional help for your child to help him deal with the problem. It is very crucial to get the right kind of help.

The right help at the right time can get your child back on track.

Some professionals that can help your child include your family doctor and a counselor or mental health professional. Even though they

might not admit it, your teens need your constant guidance and direction while they stumble through new experiences. How they deal with their curiosities, confusions, and stresses to a large extent depends upon the support you provide to them. Be there for your teens and help them lead a happier and healthier life free from substances.

Key Points

- ➤ Parents need to be proactive and make the Internet a fantastic resource and learning tool without harming their children.

- ➤ Life skills are essentially those that help promote mental well-being and competence in young people as they face life's realities.

- ➤ Teaching your children about handling money, banking, shopping, and cooking are the best ways you can equip them when they are about to embark upon the journey of attaining their education and will save them a significant amount of anguish.

- ➤ Clear boundaries and standards provide teens with the much-needed stability to handle relationships, roles and establish their own identities.

- ➤ Attempting to control your child's behavior by using guilt, withdrawing love, or invalidating feelings or beliefs is futile in the long run.

- ➤ An essential part of parenting is to teach our teens to identify, accept, and express their feelings in positive ways.

➢ Parents need to watch out for symptoms that indicate their child being stressed including aggression, withdrawal, physical illness, sleeplessness, depression, and drastic weight loss or gain.

➢ When you see evidence that your child is highly stressed and is resorting to substance abuse or suicide ideation, get professional help immediately.

➢ Depression affects more teens than ever, and about half of all cases of teen depression are unrecognized and untreated.

➢ One of the best things you as parents can do to help your teens is to **communicate** with them.

➢ The right help at the right time can get your child back on track.

➢ Getting the message, we are in this together across to your teenagers will help build a respectful and cooperative relationship with your adolescent.

➢ Do not make your children live your dreams. Make career decisions with and not for your child.

➢ As long as it does not interfere with their education, part-time jobs can help with your teen's overall development!

> If they know we believe in them, teen girls will believe in themselves. They will become strong, confident, and successful women.

> Parents need to talk to their teens about coping strategies, understanding and accepting their feelings, why it is okay to make mistakes, and most importantly, about how you will always be there for them.